SUCCESS is just 6 Steps Away

You have it in you
Discover yourself

Dinesh K. Vohra

JAICO PUBLISHING HOUSE

Mumbai • Delhi • Bangalore • Kolkata
Hyderabad • Chennai • Ahmedabad • Bhopal

Published by Jaico Publishing House
121 Mahatma Gandhi Road
Mumbai 400 023
jaicopub@vsnl.com
www.jaicobooks.com

SUCCESS IS JUST 6 STEPS AWAY
ISBN 81-7992-275-8

First Jaico Impression : 2004
Second Jaico Impression : 2004

Printed by:
Efficient Offset Printers
215, Shahzada Bagh, Industrial Complex,
Phase - II, Delhi- 110035

To my parents and elders
who had been a constant source
of inspiration to me and my family

The Making of Success is just six steps away

Dear readers

Life is an arduous journey and my personal experience has not been any different. I can easily match my 'life swings' to a ping-pong ball. A question has always tormented me as to what fails us. As a human being, we have the best of brains, skills and analytical abilities and despite that we fail to overcome the change, challenges and adversities. Since time immemorial, man has been in search of peace, happiness and success but very few have succeeded in understanding the real meaning of true success. I have known many people messing up their lives in the quest of success and happiness. I genuinely feel for those, who lose track of life and invite all kinds of anxieties, worries and stresses. It leads to anger, disappointment and frustrations. How can we get away from this mess-up?

In my experience, most people have big dreams but lack the courage, passion, determination, discipline and commitment to convert them into reality. Some people rely solely on their fate, luck or destiny and fail to make enough efforts to take them far. This brings only misfortune and consequently leads to deep frustration. True success is not the consequence of a few isolated efforts. It is a complete and holistic process, which deals with your body, heart, mind and soul.

Friends, my self-discovery has been a great revelation and it has changed my outlook towards life totally. The consequence of this change has been really pleasant and joyful. This comfort had its source in self-examination or a kind of self-questioning. I wonder why did I not examine myself earlier? But then how many people indulge in self-examination? Very few, I think. This perspective has compelled me to share my delightful experience with the readers of this book.

This book is a self-help reference book that can be repeatedly referred to if you are in a state of doubt, dilemma or confusion. This is not a 'one time read' book. It deals with all the obstacles one faces with on the way to success. It offers concrete and practical solutions to achieve success and live a meaningful and fulfilled life. All it requires is a right kind of emphasis on attitude and behavior training that would bring the desired changes to meet future challenges. We all must be mentally ready to expect the unexpected. I also believe that it wont be that easy to succeed in today's fast moving and unpredictable times but right kind of inputs on learning would enable the individuals and organizations to weather any kind of storms. I think we need to come out of our comfort zones and seek some kind of adventure to remain dynamic and vibrant in life. Here the role of future leadership would be of immense value. Organizational leaders would be compelled by the market dynamics to work relentlessly as social scientist to bring energy and dynamism into the entire gamut of activities inside an organization. Future leaders will have to work as motivators and catalyst for future growth, which would satisfy the individual and organizational aspirations.

Dear readers, true success would be the outcome of a perfect blending of right vision, right knowledge and right conduct. Only this blending will create mental toughness to face the market and competitive forces. It wont be proper to expect that some day these market pressures would go away. It would never happen. Those who will have the mental toughness to fight these forces would survive, thrive and prosper; others would simply flow with the current and perish. We as individuals and organizations will need to get into a new kind of thinking, belief and convictions that will transform us into responsible people who have the capability to guide our destinies towards the directions of our dreams.

Friends, as a seminar speaker, I have been speaking at various forums for many years on a wide variety of subjects that deals with peace, success and happiness in life. Having been witness to the mess up around us, I was encouraged to put my talks in words so as to benefit a large number of people, as print media has a much wider reach. This book carries the useful tools to help individuals and organizations to remain dynamic and vibrant.

During the making of this book, I got valuable assistance from many sources. I would like to offer my sincere gratitude to all those who have been associated with me, directly or indirectly, and have made a tangible contribution while writing the pages of this book. In particular, I would like to thank my wife Manjoo, daughter Divya and son Skand who supported my cause and me whole-heartedly. I am also grateful to Honey-Bee journal (www.sristi.org) for having granted me the permission to reprint two stories: 'Taking nature for granted - Naga Folk Tales by Lukhiram R, and Aaruni.' Apart from that I would like to offer my sincere thanks to all my friends, associates, superiors and peers who had helped in my cause and supported me fully.

I accept that it won't be possible for me to thank everyone in words but I am sincerely thankful to all known and unknown people who have contributed in the form of anecdotes, experiences or useful material to the cause of this book. I would be ungrateful if I don't pay my thanks to my Publishers, Jaico Publishing House and its entire team who did a painful but a marvelous job.

My friends, this book is an honest effort in the right direction and I hope that readers, young or old, will find the pages of this book interesting. The 'Action-Sheets' at the end of every chapter will help readers immensely. This book will encourage action and motivate people to convert their full potential into reality. This book in your hands clearly demonstrates that you are a winner and have taken the first step in the right direction. Simply have a belief that you can do it. You are what you think; you get what you desire.

You have it in you
Discover yourself

— Dinesh K Vohra

About the Author

Mr. Dinesh K. Vohra is a government officer and a highly qualified professional. A motivator par excellence, he has successfully conducted seminars for the corporate sector and government agencies across the country. Mr. Vohra is a science graduate and has done his MBA from the Narsee Monjee Institute of Management Studies, Mumbai University, with specialization in HRD. He also has a master's diploma in computers with specialization in systems analysis and design from NIIT. Mr. Vohra has conducted workshops on a wide variety of subjects like Positive Attitude, Self-esteem, Change Management, Leadership and Team-building, Communication and Interpersonal Skills, Success, Motivation, Goals, Values and Vision, and Stress Management. His seminars have been acclaimed by government agencies as well as corporate sector organisations. Mr. Vohra has many years' experience in conducting sessions for a wide variety of audiences in useful "behavioural concepts and aids" for personal and professional development. He has used his wide experience while writing this book.

CONTENTS

CHAPTER 1

THE POWER OF A POSITIVE ATTITUDE

Berlin Olympics, 1936. The excitement in the stadium was palpable, the atmosphere electric. Jesse Owens, one of the greatest athletes of the 20th century, was taking part in the elimination round of the long jump event. Among the audience was none other than the German Nazi Fuhrer Adolf Hitler himself, who was viewing the event from the grandstand. Owens had already won the gold in the 100 metres sprint, but was having trouble qualifying for this event: he had failed in the first two attempts. At this stage his German opponent Luz Long, ignoring all racial and competitive differences and risking action by the Nazi authorities, suggested that Owens start his jump earlier by a few inches — the American needed 23 feet 6 inches to get to the next round. Taking Luz's suggestion, Owens jumped exactly the distance required to get to the final round. Owens then went on to reach the finals, eventually beating Luz convincingly to win the gold medal. Hitler, enraged by the fact that a black man had beaten the German Luz, immediately stalked out of stadium. Luz, on the contrary, was the first one to congratulate Owens; the two in fact went on to become life-long friends.

Can there be a better example of the true Olympic spirit than Luz's gesture; the spirit that maintains that the Olympics is more than just winning medals? Can anyone say that Luz Long was a loser? Winning is all about having a positive mental attitude, great values, character and integrity.

There are three things that are essential for success — attitude, skills and knowledge. In other words, the ASK formula. Let's start with knowledge first:

Knowledge: It's a key element of success. The right kind of knowledge enables us to correctly identify facts, helping us to acquire a better understanding of the internal and external environments. Some people equate good education with good knowledge. The reality however is quite to the contrary. Good grades in examinations do not guarantee high knowledge levels: degrees or grades that have been acquired through cramming, for instance, are of little value in real-life situations. The route to true knowledge has to pass through the valleys and passes of great character, discipline, commitment and timely activation of dormant capacities, energies and intelligence. There is virtually no other way to acquire true knowledge and attain wisdom. Paulo Freire said: "Knowledge emerges only through invention and reinvention, through the restless, impatient, continuing hopeful enquiry men pursue in the world, within the world and with each other."

Skills and competencies: A skill can be described as an ability to do something or to apply a concept or idea; competence is the ability and willingness to do it. Skills and competencies are as important as knowledge and are critical components of a composite leadership development.

Attitude: Attitude is nothing but a state of mind that directs our actions in daily life. It is a kind of mental orientation. We are all products of our attitudes — whether negative or positive — and it is important to examine them from time to time to discover their real impact on our lives.

A positive attitude is the first stepping stone to success

What distinguishes successful people from the rest of the pack is a positive attitude: a positive attitude leads to positive behavior and ultimately to success. This is important if we are to optimize our potential and capacities; in a vast majority of people these remain grossly underutilized.

Dr. S. Radhakrishnan, former Indian President, while talking about people with a great attitude who had influenced our lives, once quoted a verse from the *Bhagvad Gita:* "Whatsoever a great man does, the same is done by others as well. Whatever standards he sets, the world follows." He went on to add: "Great men are path breakers who blaze the trail that other men follow. The light generally comes through individuals who are mentally advance of society. They see the light shining on the mountains while their fellows sleep in the valley below."

A positive attitude is a potent force; a negative attitude, on the other hand, prevents us from realizing our full potential. After having done an exhaustive study on successful people, I can definitely say that they reached the position they were in because they developed and maintained a positive outlook. They took charge of their lives and did not allow environmental pressures and adversities to distract them. Happiness and pain go hand in hand. As someone once said: "Life is a long series of sorrows punctuated by happiness."

Inventor Thomas Alva Edison made 10,000 attempts before he succeeded with the light bulb. Any other person would have quit the scene, but Edison refused to give up. Now people with a negative mindset might say that Edison failed 10,000 times before he succeeded. However, the fact is that Edison discovered 10,000 ways of not failing; every time Edison failed in his experiments, he learnt a lot. It is said that we learn a little when we succeed, a lot when we fail. Failure is a great learning tool; the real winners in life are those who tolerate failures and pain. Only those who are willing to take risks and lose succeed. We should not forget that stories of great successes are also the stories of great failures. If you think there is a magic mantra for success, think again. Edison had his own formula for success. According to him, (a) it takes time to achieve greatness, (b) have patience, and (c) persistence. British statesman Winston Churchill said: "Success is going from one failure to the next without a loss of enthusiasm."

A positive attitude is also the first step towards tackling everyday problems — be it personal or professional. You see everything that happens around and within you through the filter of your attitudes. Since many events are beyond your control, you can neither choose what happens to you, nor guarantee success and happiness. But you can definitely choose how you feel about these happenings or how you react to them. A positive mindset allows you to have the mental ability and the strength to be happier and take things in your stride. As the philosopher Epictetus said: "There is only one way to happiness and that is to cease worrying about things which are beyond the power of our will."

In today's fast-changing environment, most people feel that it is not so easy to succeed and move ahead. As I have said earlier, it's all about attitude. If you think you can win, the chances are that you will; if you feel that you can't, you probably won't.

A positive attitude creates positive synergies

During the past few years, I have conducted a large number of seminars and had the good fortune to meet a large number of successful people from diverse fields. I have found that, more than their knowledge or their competence, it was their positive attitude that was responsible for their success. And believe me, this attitude is contagious. These persons inspire and motivate people in their organisations, ensuring that they are more productive and energetic. A positive attitude breeds positive synergies, which makes for a firm foundation to plan your life.

Take people like Abraham Lincoln, Mahatma Gandhi, Henry Ford, Swami Vivekanand and Albert Einstein. What made them so different? What enabled them to stand out from the crowd? The answer: their character and attitude. We can learn a lot from these icons.

Take Abraham Lincoln, for instance, who had to overcome many failures before becoming a great leader:

- **He failed in business at the age of 21.**
- **He lost a legislative election at the age of 22.**
- **He lost his sweetheart at the age of 26.**
- **He lost a congressional election at the age of 34.**
- **He lost another congressional race at the age of 36.**
- **He lost the senatorial race at the age of 45.**
- **He lost the vice-presidential race at the age of 49.**

Yet, Lincoln never let these setbacks get in his way and eventually went on to become the president of the USA at the age of 52. Booker T. Washington, who was born a slave, overcame many social and economic obstacles to start one of the first educational institutions for African-Americans in the USA and became one of the country's foremost educators. He said: "I have learned that success is to be measured not so much by the position that one has reached in life as by the obstacles which he has overcome while trying to succeed."

Another example of a person who succeeded because of his positive attitude is Andrew Carnegie, who was born in a very poor family in Scotland and arrived in the United States at the age of 13. Carnegie rose from being a messenger boy in a Pittsburgh telegraph office to become the richest man in the world. At the turn of the 20th century, he sold his company Carnegie Steel for $480 million for the good of the community. Carnegie had the tremendous ability to think beyond immediate possibilities. According to him: "The rising man must do something exceptional, and beyond the range of his special department... there is no service so low and simple, neither any so high, in which the young man of ability and willing disposition cannot readily and almost daily prove himself capable of greater trust and usefulness, and, what is equally important, show his invincible determination to rise."

Keep pace with rapid changes

During the past few decades there has been a phenomenal growth and changes in technology and the social structure. The pace of change is staggering and daunting. The quantum of information is doubling almost every 20 months, forcing decision-makers to quicken the pace of innovation to remain dynamic and competitive. Vince Lombardi, one of the world's greatest soccer coaches, when asked to describe his offensive strategy in this rapidly changing world said: "To knock down all the opposing players." When asked about his defensive strategy, he retorted: "To knock down all the opposing players." He added: "If we do these two things well all our other plans fall into place." According to him, "the dictionary is the only place where success comes before work. Hard work is the price we must pay for success. I think you can accomplish almost anything if you are willing to pay the price."

Of course, if we know that we are working on the right things, our attitude is bound to remain positive. So, in times of change, challenges, confusion, rupture, turmoil and adversities, it depends upon our values, character, integrity and positive attitude whether we stick to the right path. Positive energies flow from true values.

Our conditioning or programming process is responsible for our beliefs, creating, reinforcing and cementing much of what we believe about ourselves. And our beliefs are the foundation stones on which our attitudes rest. Our beliefs determine our attitudes and create our feelings; our feelings are filters through which our actions flow. As an end result our actions determine whether we succeed or fail. Our behaviour pattern has a direct bearing on our productivity, relationships, teamwork and the quality of our personal and work life.

The great American entertainer Walt Disney was a great optimist, dreamer and visionary. He believed that "all of our dreams can come true if we have the courage to pursue them". Disney always pursued his goals vigorously and became bankrupt many times during his lifetime. One of his biggest dreams was to set up a beautiful resort/park in the US. Undeterred by the challenges Disney went ahead with the project and construction on it was soon underway. But then tragedy struck and he died before the park was inaugurated. On the day of inauguration, two executives were overheard talking to each other. Said one of them: "It's too bad Walt Disney is not alive to see all this." To which the other replied: "Walt Disney did see it. That's why you and I are here." That was the power of vision. Can it happen without having a positive mental attitude?

A positive attitude always leads to:

- **Higher productivity.**
- **Good teamwork.**
- **Good relationships.**
- **A secure feeling.**
- **High self-esteem.**
- **Trust.**
- **Pleasant personalities.**
- **Passion and optimism.**
- **Good motivation.**
- **A sense of integrity, service and contribution.**

This poem by an unknown author below beautifully sums up people with high energies, confidence and a positive attitude.

There is nothing to fear — you're as good as the best,
As strong as the mightiest, too
You can win in every battle or test;
For there's no one just like you
There's only one you in the world today;
So nobody else, you see,
Can do your work in as fine a way,
You're the only you there'll be!

So face the world, and all life is yours,
To conquer and love and live;
And you'll find the happiness that endures
In just the measure you give;
There's nothing too good for you to possess,
Nor heights where you cannot go;
Your power is more than belief or guess,
It is something you have to know

There is nothing to fear — you can and you will
For you are the invincible you,
Set your foot on the highest hill,
There's nothing you cannot do

People with a positive attitude are energetic and take initiative. They don't sit back for want of opportunities. They act and make the opportunities if they don't find one.

In fact, in my experience it is attitude that is more important than aptitude. Persons who have a positive attitude expect great things in their lives and work hard to achieve them. According to research done by psychologist Martin Seligman of the University of Pennsylvania, optimistic people are happier, healthier and more successful than those with a negative outlook. One of the pioneers in psychology, William James, said: "The greatest discovery of my generation is that human beings can alter their lives by altering their attitude of mind."

A negative attitude will leave you in the dumps

A negative attitude is usually the sum of negative habits that one has developed in the past. It can also be because of negative responses that one has built into one's system over a period of time. No bright idea or good work can come out of a negative mindset. A negative person is always finding fault instead of being productive. This attitude not only drains your energies, it lowers the morale and drive of those around you. To see how prevalent this attitude is, take a look at the negative statements we make in our everyday lives. According to a study of households conducted by Charles Thompson, parents utter 18 negative statements for every positive one, usually to an inquisitive child! Oops. You can see for yourself how many negative stories occupy the prime slot on television news channels these days. Surely it's no surprise that they far outnumber the positive ones?

A shoe company had sent sales representatives to a certain region to look for new markets. They were asked to report back to the management within a specific time period about the possibilities there. After some time they got a report from one of them. It read: "There is no scope for selling shoes as no one wears them here." The report sent by another read: "This place is a gold mine as no one wears shoes here." Similar circumstances, different perceptions. But what a difference a positive attitude can make!

Take for instance the case of call centres. During the course of the day, an executive employed in a call centre handles a large number of calls. A majority of the callers are polite and reasonable, but some are difficult to handle. It's not to say that their grievances are any different from those of other customers, it's just that their attitude that makes them difficult to deal with.

In his book, *Attitude: Your Most Priceless Possession*, Elwood N. Chapman exhorts readers to "think of your attitude as your mental focus on the outside world". He says it's "like using a camera. You can focus or set your mind on what appeals to you. You can see situations as either opportunities or failures... a cold winter day as either beautiful or ugly... A departmental meeting as interesting or boring. Quite simply, you take the picture of life you want to take."

Success: A price must be paid

Without success it is difficult to take pride in oneself. Success brings joy and excitement into our lives. There's hardly a person on this planet who doesn't want to succeed. But in my experience, not many people are willing to pay the price to become successful. That's probably the reason why winners have become like islands — few and far in between. We all wish to be successful and worship the winners but fail to ensure the commitment that is needed to put us on the highway to success. According to Andrew Carnegie: "Here is prime condition of success: concentrate your energy, thoughts and capital exclusively upon the business in which you are engaged."

A negative attitude at the workplace leads to bad behaviour, arrogance, rudeness, inactivity and creates an atmosphere of distrust. According to a survey done in 1998 by the University of North Carolina, rudeness or inactivity at the workplace adversely affects commitment, productivity, morale and the bottomline. According to the survey, 53 per cent of the respondents said they lost time worrying about the incidents, 22 per cent said they decreased their work efforts and 10 per cent conceded that they cut back on the hours they worked. Almost half the people surveyed contemplated quitting their jobs, while 12 per cent had already quit.

A negative mind-set shows itself in:

- Confusion and indecisiveness.
- Resentment.
- Lower productivity.
- Shirking of responsibility.
- Greed and selfishness.
- Fatalistic behavior.
- Lack of discipline, courage and confidence.
- Sulking nature.
- Stressful life.
- Insecurity and bitterness.
- Politics and manipulation within the organisation.
- Strained relationships.
- Fault-finding and criticism.

This story of the Mughal Emperor Akbar and his courtier Birbal shows how a negative attitude leads to undesirable results. Once Akbar asked Birbal to do his portrait. After it was finished, the portrait was shown to the other courtiers in the emperor's court and Akbar asked them if they had any suggestions. Most of the courtiers added their own brushstrokes to the painting, eventually making a mess of it. When Birbal saw the result, he was horrified. He beseeched Akbar to give the courtiers who had added their brushstrokes a canvas each, asking them to make a fresh portrait of the emperor. The result was anybody's guess.

Most of us behave like Akbar's courtiers sometimes. We assume the role of critics, irrespective of whether we are capable of making such judgements or not.

But it's not really whether we succeed or fail that matters — it is the attitude with which we face challenges and adversities that determines our happiness. It is positive attitude that enables us to communicate effectively and resolve differences and problems, no matter what they are. Albert Einstein said once: "The significant problems that we face can't be solved at the same level of thinking we were at when we created them."

Cultivating the right attitude: catching them young

We have seen how having the right positive attitude contributes to success. The process that shapes our attitudes begins in childhood and continues through adulthood. The educational process, our life experiences... all these play their part. Our parents, guardians, mentors and friends play a major role in this process.

Whatever we learn as children remains forever in our minds. Parents and teachers can help children develop a positive mental attitude.

Follow these cardinal principles while grooming children:

- **Devote ample time to the child.**
- **Show your appreciation and your caring attitude.**
- **Listen to the child and don't be irritated by the repeated questioning of an inquisitive child.**
- **Enjoy the child's activities and encourage him.**
- **Be friendly to him and tell simple stories of good morals and values.**
- **Create confidence and share your feelings and experience.**
- **Respect the child's friends.**
- **Allow the child to communicate freely without hesitation.**
- **Help the child in the process of development; don't force your wishes on him.**
- **Show him the importance of love, sharing and being courteous, humble and empathetic.**
- **Respect the interests of the child and groom him accordingly.**
- **Help the child create his own identity.**
- **And remember what Victor Hugo said: "The supreme happiness in life is the conviction that we are loved... loved for ourselves, or rather, loved in spite of ourselves."**

Don't use negative words while speaking to your kids; they could do immense harm to a child's psyche. I often ask parents, teachers and mentors to refrain from using negative words like "stupid, bad, donkey or clumsy" to the kids. Is it the way you want a kid to see himself? Isn't this kind of labelling harmful? You could hurt their psychological growth when you use such words, intentionally or unintentionally. Don't forget, these labels sometimes stick for a lifetime.

While speaking to your children, refrain from using such negatives:

- Do this.
- Don't do that.
- How did you dirty your clothes?
- Don't be so excited.
- What's wrong with you today?
- Don't play with such guys or toys.
- Don't scream.
- Let me do it right for you.
- Why aren't you concentrating on studies?

Using such negative words and rebukes will never enable children to develop confidence; ultimately they would suffer from a negative mindset and poor self-esteem. In other words, this could be a case of reaping what you are sowing. Think and deliberate before you say anything. Harsh words are like arrows out of a bow: they never come back. According to William Feather: "The big things that come our way are... the fruits of seeds planted in the daily routine of our work." Childhood influences – whether positive or negative — leave a permanent impact on a person's psyche.

The educational process, the workplace, the social and cultural environment, the media, relationships, superstitions and other experiences are all instrumental in shaping attitudes. Take for example the influence of the media. Many market surveys have concluded that most television advertisements are targeted at children. A child is easily influenced when he watches a television commercial many times. It creates a need for the product that is being advertised irrespective of its utility. If you observe the buying habits of families in supermarkets, you will find that it's the children who make the buying decisions for most products – whether it is toothpaste, chocolate or a toy. These ads condition tender minds and become a potent weapon in the hands of marketers.

What you need to do to remain positive and create passion in your life

1. Have a vision and concentrate on that

Helen Keller once said that "the most pathetic person in the world is someone who has sight but has no vision." Our success and happiness depend on asking the right questions. The right purpose provides us with a sense of direction, helping us resolve problems and overcome dilemmas.

A vision can be described as seeing things that are not immediately visible — a desired future state. A vision provides us with a purpose in life, giving it meaning and direction. This realization leads to maturity and an understanding of our responsibility to ourselves, our family, our community, our organisation and our souls. When we fail to identify what is right for us, we move into the wilderness, torn by confusion and dilemmas. A dilemma means we have two choices and we want both, which is not possible. Mental chaos is the result of not being clear in our minds about what we want.

Some common dilemmas:

- **Creating a balance between personal and professional lives.**
- **Peace and happiness versus financial success.**
- **How to unleash creativity and resourcefulness inside organisations, which neither need them nor have been put to the test.**

- **How to create security amid rapid change.**
- **How to create an atmosphere of trust inside organisations where people operate with scarcity mentality and hidden agendas.**
- **How to maintain control, while delegating responsibility at the same time.**

Our inner strengths — character, integrity and values — help us to overcome these dilemmas. They help us stay focused.

How often do we examine our focus? Not often. Keeping things in focus gives us the power to qualitatively change the way we feel, think and live. When you drive a vehicle, what is your focus? Aren't you totally focused and manoeuvre the vehicle skillfully? Do you also think about other things simultaneously? Not really. There is always a need to examine your focus and change it from negative to positive. Examine whether you are focusing on pain or pleasure. You get what you focus on.

Cricketing icon Sachin Tendulkar is a perfect role model for millions of young people, who are dazzled by his talent, his money and his power. Tendulkar's achievements in the field of cricket are indeed extraordinary. But how did he develop that extraordinary passion for the game? Tendulkar developed his cricketing skills through persistence and his infinite capacity to take pains. He was not a natural genius, but had successfully identified the seed of genius within him and nurtured it through hard work, commitment and passion. It's his intense focus, honesty, discipline and burning desire to excel that have made what he is today. He excels when chips are down, and is an excellent example of a homegrown product of uncompromising excellence, tested by fire in the most trying and hostile circumstances. This is the hallmark of a quality man.

All you need is talent, self-belief, an unflinching capacity to work, depth of character to overcome defeat as well as victory while remaining true to your vision.

Examine your focus by answering these questions:

- **What exactly do I want from my life? — Be specific & focused**
- **Why do I want what I want? — Get rid of dilemmas**
- **How would I feel after accomplishing my goal? — Thrills or Pains**
- **Are my accomplishments in conformity with my core values? — Clarity of vision**
- **Do I feel passionate and deeply emotional about the desired outcome? — Meaningfulness & value for existence**

These questions work as powerful tools, which can define our future with greater predictability.

Even if you are highly focused, never lose sight of the surrounding environment. Thales was a Greek philosopher, mathematician and astronomer. One night, while walking down the street, he was so engrossed in observing the stars that he fell into a ditch. An elderly woman helped him out and after recognizing him, said: "Here is a person who would study the stars but cannot see what lies below his feet."

2. Action is definitely better than reaction: Be proactive

There are two kinds of people in this world: those who take responsibility and act and those who only react. On an average, majority of people react whereas only few act. People who react fail to take responsibility. They develop a negative mindset and fail to take initiative in their lives.

People who take responsibility control their lives and hence their destinies. They don't blame luck, destiny or the external environment when they fail and are driven by their own values rather than the behaviour of other people. Proactive people take initiative and look beyond the immediate. They have the will, determination, discipline, commitment, passion and courage to pursue their dreams. People who react, on the contrary, are driven by others' feelings, behaviour and the external environment.

One great man who believed in acting rather than reacting was Mahatma Gandhi. During the freedom struggle, he acted while the British raj reacted. People usually react to events taking place in society and have their own ideas about what should be done when things go wrong. However, whether they actually act on their ideas is another matter altogether; there is no congruence between what they say and what they do. When, for example, a road accident takes place, most people choose to simply go about their business instead of helping the injured person. Take the work culture in many organisations. Don't you find a lot of gossips in every organisation? Aren't hard workers always in a minority? Isn't it a fact that the vast majority of people in India and the developing world have a laid-back attitude? How can you expect to succeed with such a mindset and such an attitude?

Being proactive does not imply being pushy or overly aggressive. It's about having more initiative, more enthusiasm, a positive outlook and willingness to take responsibility. Initiative is conducive to invention and innovation; energy reserves are put to work and wonders begin to happen. A US jigsaw puzzle firm once arranged a brainstorming session to develop a new puzzle. One of the participants had gone to see an exhibition on the Egyptian Pharaoh Tutankhamun's treasure in the city. While looking at the patterns of the Pharaoh's gold mask, a new idea for a puzzle struck him like a bolt of lightning. This unique product went on to become a huge success, breaking all previous sales records. A clear case of innovation due to proactive behaviour led to bottomline gains.

Perhaps one of the best examples of a proactive individual making it to the top of the corporate ladder is software tycoon Bill Gates. In November 2002, when Gates visited Bangalore to address IT professionals, the host at the meet began by saying: "Bill Gates needs no introduction, so let me introduce the audience to him." Indeed, the number of pages in this book would be insufficient to detail everything about the phenomenon called Bill Gates. Bill Gates is known for his ambition, intelligence, the spirit of adventure and a desire to empower people. He represents the power of the idea, and has empowered billions of people with computing skills. In fact he has practically changed the face of computing; Microsoft and Windows do not require any introduction. Gates' vision is that of a connected world with devices of all kinds talking to one another. He believes that the next decade would be a digital one and will change the face of the world. Gates is a perfect role model for a whole generation of young people for his innovation, inventiveness and enterprise. Despite being the richest person on this planet, his motivation and enthusiasm make one feel as if he was trying to make his first million. What a spirit and attitude!

3. Be upbeat in your thinking

Have you ever monitored your thoughts? In general, people don't feel the need to do it. But it is a powerful tool to remain positive, upbeat and energetic. This way you can examine yourself and work on your thought processes. If you monitor your thoughts on a regular basis, you will be able to identify negative streams in your mind and consequently make efforts to eliminate them. Upbeat thinking requires paying constant attention to the flow of thoughts. The more you think about upbeat things, the more you become an upbeat person overall.

Negative thoughts detrimental to upbeat thinking:

- I can't recollect.
- It's no use.
- I don't have enough time.
- I am too shy.
- Things are not happening the way I want them to.
- I am not that fortunate.
- I am not good at math.
- I don't have a good memory.
- Nothing right ever happens to me.
- I am always overworked in the office.
- I feel depressed.
- It's impossible.
- I hate my job.
- If only I was smarter.
- If only I had more money.
- No one likes me.
- I am totally out of place.

Think of the number of times we use these words every day. Negative thoughts won't help create a positive attitude and upbeat thinking. They only drain your energies and consequently make your life stressful and miserable.

Dancer Sudha Chandran is physically challenged. She overcame her innumerable problems and huge physical handicap to become a classical dancer of repute. She programmed her mind in such a way that she could do extraordinary things. It's all in our minds.

4. Take time off to relax, meditate and enjoy life

After a day of hard work, our body need rest. In today's rapidly changing environment, it has become increasingly difficult to create a balance between family and work life. Hectic schedules and tight deadlines leave far less time for our personal life. To keep fit and relaxed, regular relaxation and exercise are mandatory. A good night's sleep of seven-eight hours is necessary for physical and mental fitness. Over-exertion and tight schedules lead to undue anxieties and fears and cause early burn-outs. Physical disorders and heart problems in young people are on the rise, a clear indication of fatigue and over-worked bodies. Is there a way out of this mess? What can we do?

How to be relaxed and stress-free:

- **Don't concentrate on negative things.**
- **Refrain from undue criticism.**
- **Get more organised.**
- **Manage your time better.**
- **Don't let the external environment take control of your life.**
- **Take control of your feelings, emotions, needs and attitudes.**
- **Treat yourself well.**
- **Show empathy towards people.**
- **Control your habits — food, drinking, smoking etc.**
- **Concentrate on what is necessary instead of what is not urgent.**
- **Exercise on a daily basis and meditate.**
- **Be joyful and humorous.**
- **Think of people whose lives are more painful than yours.**

Daily exercise and a balanced diet are essential ingredients for a positive outlook. A healthy body and healthy mind keeps us in high spirits. It's not easy to have a positive attitude if we feel sick and unhappy. It's entirely up to us how we face circumstances — either in a positive way or in a negative fashion. I have not read about or come across a truly successful person who had a poor attitude.

It's also important to be energetic and enjoy life. Another important facet of successful people is that they enjoy life. Have you ever noticed that many scientists love music and are actively involved in the creative arts? A lot of them play musical instruments as well. Albert Einstein, for example, could play Mozart eloquently on the violin; music helped him to think and sort out his theorems in physics. Creative pursuits relax the mind and bring new vitality and energy to one's life. George Ingle Finch, a British chemist, attained great heights — literally and metaphorically — in mountaineering, climbing several peaks in Europe, especially in the Alps. In 1922, he even went on an expedition to Mount Everest. American inventor John Fitch, who invented the steamboat, loved poetry. Here's a sample of his poetry:

Song of the Brown Jug

With my jug in one hand and my pipe in the other
I'll drink on my neighbour and friend,
All my cares in a whiff of tobacco I'll smother,
My life I know shortly must end

I'll ne'er trouble myself with the cares of my nation,
I've enough of my own to mind
All we see in this world is but grief and vexation,
To death I am shortly resigned

So we'll laugh, drink, and smoke
And leaving nothing to care,
And drop like a pair ripe and mellow,

When cold in my coffin, I'll leave them to say
'He's gone, what a true hearted fellow.'

Life is meant to be happy and fulfilling. Doing things from your heart brings joy and success. Many decades back, a survey was conducted of people who wished to be millionaires. After a gap of twenty years, when the same people were surveyed again, it was found that less than 10 per cent of the respondents listened to their hearts and did what they really wanted to do. The rest did jobs they did not really enjoy doing. While those who listened to their hearts became millionaires and enjoyed doing what they were doing, the others simply struggled and were highly dissatisfied with their lives. They could neither become millionaires nor could they enjoy their lives. It is of paramount importance that you choose a job or career that offers you the maximum satisfaction, joy, excitement, challenges and avenues for growth. If you don't take care of your own happiness, no one else will. You deserve the good things in life and they don't have to cost a lot.

5. Get started, persist and persevere

Act now. Sir Thomas Buxtan once said: "With ordinary talent and extraordinary perseverance, all things are attainable." Successful people are those who act. The world is full of dreamers but dreams remain just dreams if they are not realized by an action plan. Winners act on their dreams and create an action plan to make them a reality. They are quick to grasp the opportunity when it knocks on their door. They are learners and work hard in whatever activity they are engaged in.

If you need to do something on an immediate basis, simply do it. When we say things like "I really should..." or "I need to do something", it is accompanied by a feeling of anxiety caused by not having done it. Life is too short for procrastination. Get on with the work at hand and complete it before you embark on another task. Each day brings forth an opportunity to start afresh and make life fulfilling. As someone once said: "No one can predict to what heights you can soar; even you will not know until you spread your wings." So get ready to spread your wings.

Take calculated risks. Real winners never wait for all the lights to turn green because that never happens. They get off the block at the first opportunity. Getting started is the first step in the direction towards fulfilling your dreams. Winners prepare hard in advance and plan properly. Someone once said: "If you fail to plan, you plan to fail." Successful people are risk takers and make their own opportunities. According to George Bernard Shaw, "The people who get on in this world are people who get up and look for the circumstances they want and, if they can't find them, make them." Success is reserved only for those who dare to venture into unknown territories. People who act see the positive in people, situations and opportunities and act accordingly. Those who risk nothing in life, risk everything." But think and deliberate carefully before you jump the gun. A blind jump may land you into mental, physical and financial misery.

Take the case of the two frogs that dwelt in the same pool. One day they found their pool fast drying up and decided to find some other watery home. On their search, they came across a deep well with ample amount of water. Said one to the other: "Let's make this our home as it has enough shelter and food for us." The other replied with caution: "Suppose this well dries up too? Then there won't be a way out of it. It would be impossible to climb out." The moral of the story: do nothing without considering the consequences.

Ethiopian athlete Abebe Bikila, considered the greatest marathoner of all time, was born in a very poor family and joined the army to earn his living. He was spotted by Swedish trainer Onni Niskanen, who then undertook to train him. With patience, ability and foresight the coach transformed the rough diamond into a finely cut sparkling jewel. Running barefoot, Bikila stunned the world by winning the gold medal in the marathon event at the 1960 Rome Olympics. And despite having undergone an appendicitis operation a month before, this brave athlete, with amazing perseverance, went on to win another marathon gold at the 1964 Tokyo Olympics. Few people may be aware that Bikila had also participated in the 1968 Mexico Olympics even though he had a hairline fracture in his right foot. He took part in the race just to motivate his fellow countryman who was taking part in the event. Acute pain forced him to drop out at the 17 kilometre stage, but by that time he had succeeded in what he had set out to do: his team-mate was inspired enough to win another gold for his country. There can't be a better example of will, planning, courage, commitment and perseverance. Imagine running with a fractured foot! Only such persons create history. The others merely follow the current and watch things happen. They don't make things happen. Can you identify an Abebe Bikila inside you?

Respect time. Winners always do it in time and that's probably why they never lose. They never wait for tomorrow because tomorrow never comes. Yesterday is history, tomorrow is a mystery, and today is a gift of God, the reason why it's called present. Procrastinators have the habit of perennially postponing the things, be it for days, weeks, months or years. They lament and wait for the perfect day and time to do a job and spend their lifetime in waiting. Nothing tangible ever happens for them.

Think of people who postpone things indefinitely on one

pretext or the other. Do you think they would ever find a reason to do anything? There can be never a perfect time or day. A day is a day and one must begin to succeed. The Chinese saying that "a journey of a thousand miles begins with a single step" makes a lot of sense. Those who sit on the shore waiting for a bonanza go back empty-handed. Procrastinators make New Year resolutions, only to break them the very next day. Procrastination has never helped anyone. It is a negative habit whose end result is only misfortune. Never curse the darkness; if possible light a candle.

If you wish to succeed, don't expect anyone to deliver opportunities to your doorstep. Nothing happens by accident; you have to go out and make it happen. Action is the key word here. You are capable of doing amazing things and only you have the capacity to fulfill your dreams. Your actions are a potent force that can literally change your life. Have faith in yourself and strive to do the best. Take the responsibility and act now.

Thomas Edison was a workaholic, and hated to postpone things. One day, finding that a task was still not accomplished, he locked the doors of his laboratory and refused to allow the people who were working for him to go home until it was done. The workers' wives tried to sneak in food and other necessities and pleaded with Edison to release their husbands. But Edison didn't relent until the job was completed. Only those with such a passion for time and work become wonders like Edison. As Benjamin Franklin, the American philosopher, journalist and scientist, once said: "Never leave till tomorrow that which you can do today."

True winners respect time and manage this resource effectively. They realize that time is limited and fleeting. Losers feel that they have too little time today but would have a lot of it the next day. We can control our lives if we can identify and eliminate time wasters. In the organisational context, we must manage time to become more efficient.

Making the most of your time in the office:

- **Analyse the workload in your personal and professional lives.**
- **Get reorganised and prioritise tasks according to their importance and urgency.**
- **Delegate work as much as possible to lessen your load and save time. Delegation of responsibilities also adds value to subordinates.**
- **Handle paperwork efficiently as it is a time-consuming affair. Cumbersome paperwork hampers the decision-making process.**
- **Be efficient while dealing with people in scheduled and unscheduled meetings. Meetings consume lot of time. Avoid wasteful communication.**
- **Avoid time-wasters like too many telephone calls, uncalled-for visitors and unnecessary gossips at the workplace.**

Good time management offers many benefits in the form of greater control, improved productivity and better team-work.

Persevere at all costs: Author Thomas Carlyle had just finished writing a new book on the French revolution, after years of toil. The book was doubly important to him since he had also no money and was living in poverty. He gave the manuscript of the book to his friend John Stuart Mill for his comments. But one day, Mill's maidservant used the script to light a fire. When Carlyle heard of this, he was aghast and horrified; years of toil and thought had just gone up in smoke. But he did not wring his hands and curse fate. He rewrote the entire book from start to finish. It's only such perseverance that makes a winner.

It's true that taking risks and perseverance causes lot of pain, but then most pleasures can be had only after suffering acute pains. Childbirth is an extremely painful experience for a mother but eventually the child brings immense delight not only to her but to everyone else as well. This poem exemplifies this philosophy of action, perseverance, pain and the ensuing pleasure.

Lessons from an Oyster

There once was an oyster
Whose story I tell,
Who found that some sand
Had got into his shell

It was only a grain,
But it gave him great pain,
For oysters have feelings
Although they're so plain

Now, did he berate
The harsh workings of fate,
That had brought him
To such a deplorable state

Did he curse at the government
Cry for election,
And claim that the sea should
Have given him protection

'No,' he said to himself
as he lay on a shell,
Since I cannot remove it
I shall try to improve it

Now the years have rolled around

As the years always do,
And he came to his ultimate
Destiny stew

And the small grain of sand
That has bothered him so,
Was a beautiful pearl
All richly aglow

Now the tale has a moral
For isn't it grand,
What an oyster can do
With a morsel of sand

What couldn't we do
If we'd only begin,
With some of the things
That got under our skin

— *Author Unknown*

In order to achieve something, you need the attitudes and habits that keep you on the right track. Getting started on time is a habit. If you have begun something, persist with that. Persistence means taking a 'never say die' approach. Our resolve may weaken at times, but that shouldn't force us to deviate from our efforts. According to Steve Case: "I want to find people who have had to work hard and who have learned from their failures. Perseverance is no guarantee you'll succeed, but without it, it's almost guaranteed that you won't." There is virtually no substitute for hard work. Charles Schwab once wrote in a magazine that "it doesn't take big brains to succeed in business... I have always felt that the surest way to qualify for the job just ahead is to work a little harder than anyone else on the job one is holding down." According to Helen Keller, "I am only one, but still I am one, I cannot do everything, but still I can do something; and because I cannot do everything I will not refuse to do something that I can do."

6. Don't think only of yourself. Do something for others too

Danny Thomas said: "All of us are born for a reason, but all of us don't discover why. Success in life has nothing to do with what you gain in life or accomplish for yourself. It is with what you do for others.'

Androcles the slave escaped from the clutches of his cruel master and fled to the jungle. While he was wandering in the jungle, he came across a lion. Terrified, he took to his heels. After a while however, he noticed that the lion made no attempt to chase him. He then noticed why. The lion was injured: its paw was swollen and bleeding. Androcles took pity on the lion and bandaged its injured paw, and the lion licked his hand out of affection and gratitude. He spent some time with the lion inside a cave.

Shortly afterwards, Androcles and the lion were captured. Androcles was sentenced to be thrown into the lion's cage. The lion was kept hungry for several days and one fine day the king and his courtiers came to see the spectacle of Androcles being ripped open by the lion in the cage. But to their amazement something extraordinary happened. Instead of tearing him to pieces the lion, which recognized the friend who had treated his wounds, began licking his hand. The shocked king immediately ordered Androcles to be brought to him. After hearing Androcles' story the king was so moved that he set him free, and the lion was returned to his abode. Believe me, good deeds do pay. You don't need to wait for long. Gratitude is the sign of a noble soul.

Gratitude creates a pleasant sensation within us and gives us emotional satisfaction. Doing good satisfies our psychological needs, and noble feelings eliminate greed, envy, worry and fear from our minds. It reminds us that we don't live alone. No one likes to live like an island. Gratitude helps us to see ourselves as a part of a benevolent system. As Albert Einstein said: "A hundred times every day, I remind myself that my inner and outer life depends on the labours of other men, living and dead, and that I must exert myself in order to give in the measure as I have received and am still receiving."

When we show our gratitude in words and action — that is by saying thanks, paying tributes, accepting mistakes gracefully or helping out a needy person — we are rewarded with a feeling of goodness. God has blessed all of us with a capacity to help others and to be benevolent towards all.

Edison was taught telegraph skills by a grateful employer for saving his son. One day the three-year-old son of the stationmaster wandered on to the railway tracks while a train hurtled towards him. Without giving a thought to his own safety, Edison saved the life of the little boy. We all know Edison as a great scientist and inventor, but he was also a fine human being.

Our minds govern our bodies. British computer pioneer Charles Babbage was suffering from a severe toothache. While walking in the garden, he stumbled upon a gold coin. Excited, he started making enquiries about this find. The coin was eventually found to be made of brass, but in the excitement of the discovery Babbage had completely forgotten his toothache. According to him, one forgets the pain if one's mind is filled with pleasure. Thereafter, whenever he felt pain, he would read novels like Don Quixote or Robinson Crusoe.

One of the best ways of earning respect is by taking into consideration others' opinions. Being kind to others never causes pain. Rather, it gives joy. Some boys who were playing near a pond saw a number of frogs in the water. Thinking it would be fun, they started pelting stones at them. In the process, the children injured many frogs and killed quite a few. One of the frogs, lifting his head out of the water, cried out: "Please stop, dear boys. What is sport and fun to you is death to others." One man's pleasure can be another man's pain. Compassion is the best form of gratitude.

Sometime back, I was watching the live telecast of a cricket match. One of the batsmen hit a beautiful stroke and as the ball whizzed along to the boundary, it hit a bird. It was a painful sight. To my astonish-ment, most of the players ran towards the bird, which was immediately rushed for treatment. After some time the state of the bird's health was announced. This might appear to be a small incident, but it conveys a strong message. We might be involved in big projects, but a warm attention to such things even for a few moments gives us relief from present anxieties, worries and stresses. A sense of contribution adds significant value to our lives.

I was recently reading Buddha's Jataka tales. These are the stories of his previous births in animal form before he was born as Buddha, the enlightened one. One of these stories, of compassion and gratitude, touched me immensely. I would like to share this story with my readers.

Buddha in the Deer Park

It is believed that Buddha went through many incarnations in animal form before he was born as a human in the form of Prince Siddhartha of the Sankhya clan. This story is about Buddha's life as the king of the deer in a deer park.

Buddha was born in a deer park that belonged to Brahamadatta, king of Varanasi. The deer park was

Brahamadatta's favourite hunting ground, and had two groups of deer — the Banyan group and the Branch group, each comprising 500 deer. Buddha, the golden deer, was the king of the Banyan group.

During his hunting trips Brahamadatta used to ride through the park bow in hand, scattering the frightened deer hither and thither. In the scramble to get away from the king's bow and save their lives, many used to suffer injuries and some lost their lives. The king enjoyed the sight of the frightened deer scrambling to get away. Life became so miserable for the deer that the two deer kings called a meeting of all the deer to think of a way to solve the problem.

The Banyan King or Buddha said: "Friends, King Brahamadatta has made our lives miserable. He rides through the park every day and we are losing our members at an alarming rate. What we should do is that each group should send one of its members every alternate day to the king. This way King Brahamadatta will have his meat and we will be spared this daily torture." The proposal was sent to the king, who happily accepted the offer. But he put forth a condition: the two beautiful king deer were never to be killed (the king acknowledging royalty).

Each day, as planned, a deer from one group was sent to King Brahamadatta for execution. One day, it was the turn of a doe from the Branch group to be sent to Brahamadatta. She went to the king of the Branch group and said: "O lord, please put off my turn for execution as I am pregnant. I'm sure the gracious king would not like to kill two lives at once. I will take my turn after the fawn is born." However, the king of the Branch deer refused her request. He said: "The rules cannot be broken and excuses of this kind will not be accepted. It is your turn and you have to go. Asking someone else to take your place would be totally unjust."

The doe then went to the Banyan king and pleaded with him to save her unborn child. The Banyan king was moved and decided to take her place at the chopping block. When King Brahamadatta's people arrived at the chopping block for the daily slaughter, they were astonished to see the Banyan king there. They rushed back to Brahamadatta to convey the news to him. King Brahamadatta immediately rushed to the spot in his chariot and asked the Banyan king: "Did I not tell you that king deer would never be killed? Why have you come here?" The Banyan king replied: "A pregnant doe from another branch came to me and pleaded that she be allowed to take her turn at the chopping block later as she was to deliver her baby shortly. Now, it was impossible for me to turn down her request. Instead of asking someone else, I decided to take her turn."

King Brahamadatta's heart melted when he heard of the immense sacrifice made by the Banyan king. He ordered that there should be no more killing in the deer park. This way the Bodhisattva (Buddha) transformed the life of King Brahamadatta.

This is an extraordinary tale of compassion, love and sacrifice. Can there be a higher religion than this? Why can't we all emulate Buddha and make this planet a better and beautiful place in every sense?

Power of gentleness and persuasion: Gentleness and friendliness are different facets of a sense of service. It deals with your soul or the spiritual aspects of life. It defines your wholeness and integrity, and helps you feel that your life, and that of others, matters. The forces of sacrifice, love and gentleness are far greater than those of brutality and oppression.

There is a beautiful fable about the sun and the wind. The sun and the wind were arguing as to who was more powerful. Spying an old man sitting on a bench, they agreed that whoever succeeded in taking off the old man's clothes would be more powerful. The wind huffed and puffed and tried to take away the old man's clothes by sheer force. But the harder the wind blew, the tighter the old man clutched his clothes to himself. Then it was the sun's turn. The sun shone in all its glory. After a while the old man felt warm and took off one article of clothing, and then yet another until it was so hot that he undressed and jumped into a pool to cool off. The sun told the wind that gentleness and friendliness are always stronger than fury and brute force.

One day Ralph Waldo Emerson, the American philosopher and writer, and his son were trying to get a calf into a barn. They pushed hard, but the calf dug in his hooves and refused to move. An Irish housemaid saw their predicament. She was not educated but knew the language of love and persuasion. She put her finger into the calf's mouth and let it suck her finger, gently leading it into the barn. Persuasion is definitely better than any force.

There's no better way of forgetting your worries than by helping someone in need. When you think of somebody else's pain and problems, your focus is totally changed. Your outlook becomes a lot more positive and your attitude is enriched. According to Albert Pine: "What we do for ourselves dies with us. What we do for others and the world remains immortal."

We cannot help ourselves without helping others,
We cannot enrich our lives without enriching others,
We cannot prosper without bringing prosperity to others.

— Jannette Cole

7. It's important to have high self-esteem

Writer Goethe wrote: "The greatest evil that can befall man is that he should come to think ill of himself." Goethe accepted this truth about human nature. We are not defeated because we lack talent or ability; it's the lack of confidence that brings about our downfall.

It's all about self-esteem: the way we feel about ourselves. To say things like "I am wrong", "I am incompetent", or not being sure of oneself is a clear sign of poor self-esteem. When we feel good, we make extra efforts to gain knowledge or expertise and search for effective ways to handle given tasks. Feeling good keeps us buoyant and energetic and is conducive to a mental make-up that can find solutions to problems. We begin to look at problems as challenges and consequently convert threats into opportunities.

People with poor self-esteem tend to shirk their responsibilities. They stick to set limits and never explore new frontiers, remaining happy inside their comfort zones. They also try to get the most with the least effort and use short cuts, quick fixes or make cosmetic changes. They usually end up in the company of their own kind, that is, people with scarcity mentality and hidden agendas.

High self-esteem and pride: High self-esteem is directly related to personal happiness and satisfaction. However, some people confuse the terms high self-esteem and pride; there is a subtle difference between the two. While self-esteem deals with inner convictions, values, self-worth and self-respect, pride is concerned with specific achievements or actions. Pride is also a positive self-experience. We do take great pride in our achievements or those of our national sports teams at international events. When our team wins, we feel a great sense of pride. Taking pride in something wrong or negative breeds arrogance and egotistic behavior. We must refrain from self-glorification that comes at the cost of others.

Bring up children properly: How we are brought up as children also affects our self-esteem; if children are brought up properly, they develop high self-esteem, which helps them face any challenges or constraints. But there are many ways in which we can go wrong while rearing children.

Take a situation where a child notices that his mother is worried because of some problem. The child notices that his mother is disturbed and asks her what the matter is. The mother, trying to protect the young one, gives a vague answer, as if nothing was wrong. The child persists in its questioning, and when it does not get a satisfying answer, starts feeling uneasy and disturbed. Meanwhile, the father of the child, who is witness to the entire scene, gets angry and asks his son not to bother his mother.

Treating a child in such a way will lead to ambiguity and doubts in his mind. Not only were his simple questions unanswered, his concerns too were ignored by the parents. Do you think that such treatment will help kids develop a healthy and confident attitude? This way, parents do more harm than good even though they may have very good intentions. Knowingly or unknowingly, they harm their ward and his mental development. Think of the exhortations made to a young child. Isn't this a bad way to bring up a child? Are you really helping your child to become a confident and dynamic person?

There are opportunities in threats: It is an acknowledged fact that people with high self-esteem are more productive, caring, humble, courageous and assertive. They accept responsibility and act accordingly. They also turn adversity into opportunity. How else how could a deaf Beethoven have created such great musical symphonies? John Milton was blind but that did not prevent him writing beautiful poetry. And cricketer Bhagvat Chandrashekhar became the finest googly bowler in the world despite a polio-afflicted arm. Such people feel good about themselves and make the best use of opportunities. They don't lament about their physical inadequacies and handicaps.

Look for virtues in others: Benjamin Franklin was not so diplomatic in his youth but was more savvier in later life. Once when he was asked about the secret of his success, he said: "I will speak ill of no man... and speak all the good I know of everybody."

One way of feeling good is to read good biographies and associating with positive people who are uplifting, upbeat, optimistic and adventurous. People with high self-esteem avoid conflicts and backbiting and focus on good and positive things. The words that you use can make or break relationships; a negative comment or communication can damage your individual or professional reputation. Don't allow your destiny to be controlled by others. Eleanor Roosevelt, wife of US president Franklin D. Roosevelt, once said: "No one can make you feel inferior without your consent".

The quality of courage: 25 May 2001 was a historic day for mankind. Eric Weihenmayer became the first blind man to reach the summit of Mount Everest. Weihenmayer, who lost his vision at the age of 13, never let his blindness interfere with his passion for mountaineering. He has shown such charm, resilience, passion, commitment and concern for others that it is difficult to find a better role model. In his book Touch the top of the world — the story of his conquest of the highest peaks in the world — Weihenmayer showed the world that the barrier of blindness can be overcome if one has the will and courage to do it. According to Helen Keller, "Avoiding danger is no safer in the long run than outright exposure. Life is either a daring adventure, or nothing."

Courage is the quality of qualities. Without this quality, all other qualities have no value. True courage has its origin in truth and ethical practices, at whose core lie universal principles. It can be derived from the inner self only. When every other light goes out, it is this inner light that shows us the path. It enlightens us, and gives us strength, character and mental toughness. Most of life's battles are won first at the mental level; physical victory is then a mere formality.

Cultivate optimism: People with high self-esteem have vast reserves of optimism. Kentucky Fried Chicken is one of the most well-known and successful fast food chains in the world. It wasn't always so. Colonel Sanders, founder of KFC, had to drive from door to door, town to town, to sell his first pieces of chicken. The only response he got initially was 'NO' — more than a thousand times. Now, can you imagine the faith, patience, persistence and perseverance required to withstand refusal more than a thousand times? Sanders was a great optimist and firmly believed in himself and his product; he also had the courage to persevere.

Colonel Sanders' Success Recipe:

- **Never quit.**
- **Always believe in yourself.**
- **Be patient.**
- **Be positive.**

Says Dr Robert Conoroy: "Cultivate optimism by committing yourself to a cause, a plan or a value system. You'll feel that you are growing in a meaningful direction, which will help you rise above day-to-day setbacks." Author E.M. Forster said: "One person with passion is better than forty people merely interested."

Optimists always have something to look forward to. You feel good if you are expecting mail or an important communication. You look forward to holidays, vacations, birthdays or weekends or some special events. The reality may not be all that thrilling but the anticipation is far more happening and satisfying. We should not forget that life is short. Do we have enough time to concentrate on life's negative aspects? Look back with no regrets; always look forward with hope and optimism. Never be afraid of minor setbacks; just let them roll off your back.

Be patient: When it is a question of career or happiness in personal life, you'll do well being patient. Quick fixes, short cuts and a slapdash approach may work for some time but it's not sustainable in the long run. The law of nature operates in everything we do. A child for instance has to develop naturally over time; the process cannot be foreshortened. Similarly, crop cultivation has to be based on natural laws; you cannot expect crops to grow faster than what nature had intended them to. If you ask someone who has never done push-ups to do a hundred all at once, he won't be able to do it. It requires tremendous patience and sustained practice.

A famous athlete who had just won an international race was congratulated by someone who said: "You were lucky to win the race". The athlete was furious and shot back: "I practiced ten hours a day for fifteen years without a single day off, and you call it luck."

People with high self-esteem also stay away from negative influences. Parents, teachers, mentors, guides, friends and associates have a big role to play in the total and holistic development of a person.

Ways of building high self-esteem:

- **Be conscientious.**
- **Be respectful to others.**
- **Don't be rigid.**
- **Be honest.**
- **Be an optimist and a problem solver.**
- **Be a team player.**
- **Work hard.**
- **Practice empathy.**
- **Create humour.**
- **Be grateful.**
- **Believe in your abilities.**
- **Refrain from making unfair comparisons.**
- **Make healthy criticism.**
- **Refrain from unhealthy arguments at work or home.**
- **Teach true principles.**
- **Have patience.**
- **Help children become better citizens.**
- **Communicate effectively.**
- **Use a smile to win friends.**
- **Practice what you preach.**

8. Keep learning, all the time

I believe that learning is a continuous life-long process in which one success supports future achievement. An individual needs a positive self-concept in order to learn effectively. One must acquire new knowledge, insights and skills, practice to reinforce and apply those acquisitions in more advanced ways and then demonstrate proficiency. Effective learning occurs in a non-threatening, interesting and conducive environment. The learning process does not merely include formal learning assignments, but all other experiences as well. The educational system must give equal opportunities to all individuals regardless of differences in abilities, aptitudes, and interests.

The right atmosphere enables us to:

- **Acquire knowledge and learning skills.**
- **Develop thinking, initiative, creative ability and critical judgment.**
- **Acquire productive social skills.**
- **Learn to express ourselves thoughtfully and courteously.**
- **Maintain spiritual, emotional, psychological and physical health.**
- **Set goals and make decisions.**
- **Develop the responsibility and self-discipline to work independently and do a thorough job.**
- **Use technology.**
- **Develop awareness and respect for all in a multicultural society.**

We must view life as a learning opportunity. Over a period of time, we develop specific responses to particular problems or situations. These responses or habits tend to get rigid and as a consequence we are often trapped in them. As times change old ideas and practices become obsolete, and are no longer workable and practical. Changes in the environment compel us to think differently; we have to experiment with new ideas or practices to see which one will work in the changed circumstances.

We should learn from one another and shouldn't forget that the other guy may know something that we don't. We must also give a thought to how others in similar circumstances feel. We may have our disagreements but that's no reason to be discouraged. You should never feel disheartened when you fail; failing is a great learning tool.

Wise people are always eager to learn from others. They are always seeking for virtues in others. It is this quality of continuous learning that makes people wiser. I would like to share with my readers the beautiful story of King Janaka, father of Sita, when he met a sage.

Five kinds of light

This is the story of the great king Janaka, ruler of Mithila, whose daughter Sita was married to Lord Rama. One day, a venerable sage visited King Janaka's court. After making the sage feel welcome, the king asked him a question: "Where is the real and genuine source of light and how does it affect day-to-day life?"

The sage replied: "There are five kinds of light in the world. The first source of light is the sun. With sunrise, the day dawns and all activities begin. By evening, with sunset, these activities draw to a close."

"That's true," said the king. "But what lights one's way after sunset?"

"After sunset, it is the moonlight that lights our way."

"But what happens when the moon also sets?"

"Fire is the only light after the moon sets. One can work in that light," said the sage.

"If the sun and the moon have set and the fire goes out, then what lights our way?" asked the king.

"O Great King, when it's dark and nothing can be seen, our voice is the only light. We can do our work by the sound of our voice."

"That's great!" said the king. "But once the sun and the moon have set, the fire goes out and all sounds have stopped, then what would light our way?"

"Then the self alone is one's light, O Great King. It's the inner light that lights our way. Even in pitch darkness, it lights our way. This is the light of conscience and truth. This is the light of our inner self. Here you know that completeness."

This story shows amazing clarity of thought. We are enlightened when we know ourselves. The inner light helps us identify the right path. It is probably the only way to attain wisdom.

Winners never quit: Learning is all about maintaining total preparedness to succeed in life. According to Earl Nightingale, "If you are not prepared for your opportunity, when it comes, the opportunity will only make you look silly." Learners always remain physically, mentally, socially and spiritually alive and agile. They perform well because they are learners and work hard. They have an open mind, not an empty one. An empty mind is a dustbin, which does not discriminate between good and bad. American football quarterback Jeff Hostetler, formerly with the NY Giants, sat on the bench for seven years as a back-up. He got into the team when another player fell sick. He took the opportunity and led his team to a string of victories, including one in the Superbowl. Successful people are those who always keep themselves mentally and physically vigilant; consequently, they are able to take full advantage of a chance or an opportunity when it presents itself.

Most scientists and researchers have a tremendous appetite for learning and for exploring new frontiers. They also have incredible persistence, commitment and discipline.

Edison tried 10,000 times before he succeeded with the light bulb. Fast bowler Javagal Srinath remained in Kapil Dev's shadow for a long time before he made his mark in the Indian cricket team. You don't win an Olympic gold in one day. If you look at the lives of highly successful people, you will find that they overcame years of frustrations and setbacks. They succeeded because they persisted. Someone rightly said "winners never quit and quitters never win".

We should also not assume that a good formal education will ensure good judgment or good knowledge. An illiterate or less educated person too can be very knowledgeable. Take the case of Dhirubhai Ambani, creator of the Reliance empire.

Dhirajlal (Dhirubhai) Hirachand Ambani was born on the 28th of December 1932 to a schoolmaster of a local school in Chorwad (Gujarat). After doing his matriculation from a local school, Ambani began his career in Aden as a gas-filling worker. In 1958, he came back to India and started Reliance Commercial Corporation with a capital of Rs 15,000. He then went on to have his own textile mill at Naroda, Gujarat, at a cost of Rs 2.8 lakh. Thereafter he ventured into polyester filament yarn and built world-class petrochemical refineries in the nineties. His next ambition was to connect the entire country through a communication revolution. Ambani believed that this would help people overcome the handicaps of illiteracy and lack of mobility. His group's revenues in 2002 was over Rs 60,000 crore. Dhirubhai's is a story of excellence and a deep-rooted commitment to make it big. According to him, "Those who do not produce wealth discredit those who create wealth. This attitude kills the productive spirit. A society which condemns creators of wealth will always remain poor and miserable."

Here are some of his famous quotes:

"Think big, think fast, Think ahead. Ideas are no one's monopoly."

"Our dreams have to be bigger... our ambitions higher... our commitment deeper... and our efforts greater... this is my dream for Reliance and for India."

"Don't give up, courage is my conviction."

Such people create history before they themselves become history.

A good knowledge base helps us face change and the challenges of the marketplace. Building upon it from time to time is absolutely essential to remain competitive and alive. Besides, existing competencies too need to be strengthened so that we are able to face today's fiercely competitive world. It requires tremendous mental energy to bring about the changes to assume market leadership or to retain it.

It is said that knowledge is power. It's not true; knowledge is power only when it is applied. Without acting on it, knowledge is of no use. Without action or conduct, vision and knowledge are lame. Similarly, without vision, knowledge and conduct are sterile. Without knowledge, vision and conduct are blind. With right knowledge, vision and action, we can overcome most mental and physical barriers. According to British statesman Benjamin Disraeli, "Action may not always be happiness, but there is no happiness without action."

Areas of renewal: There are four areas of renewal covering different dimensions of life — the physical, mental, social and spiritual. Taking proper care of your health is of vital importance. A sick man can't enjoy life or deal with the stresses, anxieties, problems and fears of life effectively. Bad health also affects our social, mental and spiritual lives.

The mental dimension involves continuous learning and improvements in our knowledge base. Learning new technologies and strategies is necessary for survival. Why do we continuously attend training programmes? If we fail to nurture and develop leadership and team-building qualities in ourselves, we will fail to be good human beings. It is essential to acquire new competencies to remain competitive in this rapidly changing and unpredictable world.

Social learning relates to the honing of interpersonal skills. Many decades back, Dale Carnegie wrote a masterpiece called *How to Win Friends and Influence People*. Those who have not read this book must read it. It is all about people and relationships. American business tycoon John D. Rockefeller commented once that "the ability to deal with people is as purchasable a commodity as sugar or coffee. I will pay more for that ability than for any other under the sun." Effective speaking and honing communication skills improve your relationships, prestige and popularity. Everyday experiences too provide a rich source of learning.

The fourth dimension deals with our existence and spirit, about leading a balanced life. It gives our lives meaning, value and substance. Spiritual renewal — involving a sense of contribution, service and integrity — needs an investment of time. Spiritual thoughts eliminate negative thinking, ambiguities and confusion from our minds. We get focused and accomplish our task efficiently. It provides our lives with meaning and substance.

My personal experiences with people have been very enriching. In August 1990, I, along with my colleagues, had gone to visit the four holy shrines of Badrinath, Kedarnath, Yamunotri and Gangotri in Uttaranchal state in the north. These shrines are located at heights of about 10,000 feet above sea level. During our visit to Kedarnath, our group was stuck in a tiny village due to a heavy landslide for three days; the village had no hotels or dormitory accommodations and there was no way of getting to a nearby town. However, a poor villager helped us and provided us with accommodation and food for three days, though his house was barely sufficient for his own personal needs. The villager was short of food and the next morning left for a nearby village through the hills, travelling nearly 20 kilometres to buy food for us. The day we left the village, we wanted to pay extra for his fine services. However, the villager refused anything more than the cost of the food he bought for us. This is the finest example of compassion and service I have ever seen. To me such men are the true winners; they not only enrich our lives but also teach us a lesson on living an ideal life.

9. Remove the mental blocks from your life

Negative statements are huge roadblocks in our personal and professional progress. Just take a good look at these blocks and make efforts to remove them from your mindset.

Negative statements that we use every day:

- **There's only one right answer.**
- **That's not logical.**
- **Follow the rules.**
- **To err is wrong.**
- **That's not my area.**
- **That's not my responsibility.**

Such attitudes block ingenuity and resourcefulness. They also block positive synergies that could bring dynamism into our lives.

Remember the following:

- **Be a butterfly, not a crawling insect.**
- **Soar like an eagle.**
- **A turtle makes progress only when he sticks his neck out.**
- **Every success story is a story of great failure too.**
- **Every problem has an in-built solution.**
- **Every failure teaches us something.**
- **Every threat carries an opportunity.**
- **Thank God for his blessings.**
- **Count your blessings and not troubles.**
- **Begin a day with a smile.**
- **We have the power to choose and can control our thoughts.**
- **There are no hopeless situations; It is only people who become hopeless about them.**

What you should do then:

- **Be creative.**
- **Be innovative.**
- **Be inventive.**
- **Be dynamic.**
- **Be an optimist.**
- **Take initiative.**
- **Take responsibility.**
- **Have courage.**
- **Have determination.**
- **Use your ingenuity.**
- **Have a sense of humour.**
- **Create a positive synergy.**

Easier said than done. Is it really that easy to develop a positive mental attitude? Certainly not. Years of conditioning don't disappear overnight. Prejudices, biases and fixed mindsets are big barriers on the highway to success. It requires a great pull, energy and will to get away from negative influences. Those who get on in this world have a steely resolve; others merely flow with the current and perish. Don't forget that your attitude determines your altitude.

ACTION SHEET

- Think of yourself as a winner or successful person.
- Have positive expectations from whatever you do.
- Don't recollect failures; But learn from them.
- Recollect past victories.
- Associate with positive things and people.
- Keep trying and believe in the power of persistence.
- Reward yourself when you succeed.
- Be a positive listener and speaker.
- Think positive thoughts.

Now think of the instances that you have failed because of negative thinking. Find their causes. You can record such experiences below:

A —

B —

C —

D —

E —

Make a list of five positive habits that have produced positive results.

A —

B —

C —

D —

E —

You can do it; just unfold yourself. Remember what Alberta Flanders said: "Sometimes only a change of viewpoint is needed to convert a tiresome duty into an interesting opportunity." And also think of what Henry Ford said: "In my mind nothing is more abhorrent than a life of ease. None of us has any right to ease. There is no place in civilization for the idler."

CHAPTER 2

KEEP FOCUSED: DON'T LOSE SIGHT OF YOUR GOAL

The supreme goal of man is to fulfil himself as a creative, unique individual according to his own innate potentialities and within the limits of reality.

— Dr. Carl G. Jung

Guru Dronacharya was once teaching archery to his disciples, the Pandavas. He placed a wooden bird on the branch of a tree, and asked his disciples what they could see. Yudhisthira said he could see the sky, the trees, the branches and the bird. The guru was not satisfied and asked him to step aside. Then came Bhima's turn; he too gave the same answer. Finally, when Arjuna was asked what he saw, his answer was different. "I see nothing but the eye of the bird," he said. The guru was very happy with his answer and asked his pupil to shoot. And with unerring accuracy, Arjuna shot the bird through the eye. This shows what you can do if you are focused.

Harvard Business School once did a study on the differences in the success rates of people with similar backgrounds and educational standards. It found that while three per cent of people were very successful, 30 per cent were moderately so, and 67 per cent just got along. Significantly, it found that the three per cent who were very successful had written down specific goals. The 30 per cent who were moderately successful had a general idea of where they were going but did not have any formalized goals. The rest were happy to see the world go by. What is interesting is that those in the 30 per cent category needed to put in only a moderate amount of effort to get into the higher group. The secret ingredient was "the development of habits, attitudes and strategies which support the achievement of clear goals".

Why do you need a goal?

We are living today in perhaps the best time in all known human history. The opportunities and possibilities that exist for a vast number of people to realize their dreams have never been more than at the present time. With higher levels of affluence, longer life spans, and the number of options available to us, it's definitely possible to make our lives more comfortable, happy and prosperous.

A goal is a destination. You won't get very far if you walk up to a ticket counter at a railway station or bus station and simply ask for a ticket. You have to be specific about your destination. If you are unaware of your destination, how will you know when you arrive? You've got to know what your objectives are. If you jump into a car, start the engine but don't make good use of the steering wheel, you certainly won't reach your destination. So take control of the steering wheel and guide yourself forward to the destination of your choice.

A goal gives us a sense of purpose and introduces drive and passion in our lives. It is like a roadmap or compass that helps us see where we're going. In the process of setting goals, we know and identify ourselves. Goals are positive statements that can literally change our lives. According to Dr Sven Hansen, "The key to peak performance is not potential or skill, but motivation and dedication... having clear performance goals and putting in the training effort to achieve them."

People who set goals are winners with exceptional determination, commitment and application. When people set goals and achieve them they have a special glow on their faces and feel fulfilled and happy. Think of the excitement and thrill of an athlete who has won an Olympic medal. David J. Schwarz said: "Nothing happens, no forward steps are taken, until a goal is established."

According to Robert Jay Ginn Junior, "In the process of setting goals, we come to know ourselves. Virtually every cultural tradition holds among its central principle, know thyself — knowing ourselves, the capacity for reflective self-awareness, is perhaps our greatest personal achievement, at least the core one that is important to career success."

Goals can be short-term (one year), medium-term (up to three years) and long term (up to five years). Set goals in all aspects of your life.

Family or personal: Ask yourself whether you spend enough quality time with your family members. Do you meet the family's everyday needs and plan for the future?

Career and finances: Check how much money you have and how you can plan for future needs. Do you have a proper career progression plan?

Health: Do you take care of your health and exercise on a regular basis? Can you deal with mental and emotional stresses effectively?

Social and emotional: Do you deal with people with a smile and show empathy? Do you share knowledge and experience and have a helping attitude?

Psychological: Do you set aside quality time for learning? Do you read to keep yourself updated, upbeat and dynamic?

Spiritual: Do you meditate on an everyday basis? Do you have a sense of contribution, service and integrity? Ask yourself whether your goals in life are fair to people around you.

Maintain a balance in all areas of your life and ensure that your life is happy, joyful, satisfying and successful. Success is a happy by-product of your life's journey. It's not just about attaining a single goal; it is a continuous and composite onward journey. Success and failure are essential and an integral part of life. Success means different things to different people. While it may be money, fame and acclaim for some, it could be a good family and work life, community service, good health or emotional satisfaction for others. Taking a narrow view of success is likely to do more harm than good and would lead to stress and dissatisfaction. True success deals with the totality of life; it is holistic in nature.

Most professionals have an idea of what they want to achieve in their lives and professional careers, whether it's a higher sales target, a better job, an overseas journey or a promotion. However, not all people manage to achieve what they want. Even very intelligent, motivated and hard-working individuals sometimes fail to succeed. The reason is often because they fail to set clear goals and objectives. These people may have a general idea of what they want to accomplish, but the fact is that our mind does not work effectively with generalities. One has to be focused and specific as to what one wants to accomplish. Napoleon Hill said: "There is one quality which one must possess to win, and that is definiteness of purpose, the knowledge of what one wants and a burning desire to possess." Psychological surveys have also found that people who set goals in their personal and professional lives cope with problems better.

How setting goals can help you:

- **It gives you a purpose in life.**
- **Helps you make difficult decisions.**
- **Provides a sense of direction.**
- **Brings clarity and confidence to your life and resolves conflicts.**
- **Adds to self-worth and self-respect.**
- **Puts drive and passion in our life.**

The idea is to set goals to balance all of life's different aspects — personal, fiscal, physical, psychological, emotional and spiritual. An unbalanced life is the result if any one area is not given proper attention. Imagine what will happen if you work too much on social or career goals and neglect spiritual and health matters! Sure, you may earn a lot, but it'll be at the cost of your health. And the end result is that you may end up spending much of that money just to regain your lost health. Balancing all the different aspects of life is an absolute must for a meaningful and fulfilled life.

Follow these steps to examine yourself and to set right goals in life:

1. **Examine your identity, both personal and professional.** Look at your vision, purpose, attitude, self-image and beliefs. Also examine your strengths, weaknesses, opportunities and threats. According to Albert Einstein, "Imagination is more powerful than knowledge." Allow yourself to dream and desire. Without a goal, you are simply kicking a ball in a

football field with no goalpost.

2. **Define your values.** It's your values that guide your action on a daily basis, and also helps structure your life. They also affect your relationships and how you behave towards other people. The goals you set must be compatible with your value system. You are more likely to achieve them then.

3. **Where are you now?** Take a current inventory. Before you set on a journey, first take a look as to where exactly you are. If you're not aware of the starting point, how can you see how far you have progressed in your journey?

4. **Establish goals.** Establish goals in all areas of your life — family, fiscal, psychological, emotional, physical and spiritual. Set goals that are specific and which have a time frame. No one epitomized better the Renaissance Man than Leonardo Da Vinci, who is known all over the world for his superb paintings: the Mona Lisa, The Last Supper and so on. Da Vinci's interests were not restricted to art. He also excelled in engineering, architecture and science. He had developed a system to achieve goals, called the 'SMART' system.

   Goals should be:

   S – Specific.
   M – Measurable.
   A – Achievable.
   R – Realistic.
   T – Time-bound.

   Philosopher Henry David Thoreau once wrote: "If one advances confidently in the direction of his dreams and endeavours to live the life which he has imagined, he will meet with a success unexpected."

Mark Spitz, the champion swimmer of the seventies, did not start off with a big splash. When he took part in the 1968 Mexico Olympics, he was not very successful and met with bitter disappointment. But he was determined to put up a better show at the 1972 Munich Olympics. Putting the frustrations of Mexico behind him he began training with new vigour. Heat or cold, sunshine or rain — nothing deterred him. He didn't miss a single day of training; his goals had become an obsession. Then came the D-Day: the 1972 Munich Olympics. His relentless pursuit paid off — and how! Spitz won seven gold medals, creating new world records in every event he participated in.

In 1977, Spitz's name was put in the International Swimming Hall of Fame for his extraordinary achievements in the pool. His triumph was not only one of the greatest moments in US Olympic history, it showed all humankind what can be achieved through persistence, commitment and a burning desire to accomplish set goals.

5. **Anticipate problems and constraints.** What obstacles do you expect to confront that could make your job difficult to accomplish? Check out all the internal and external factors that may come in your way. Never let minor obstacles, problems or constraints upset you.

6. **What knowledge would you require to accomplish goals?** Would you need professional help, expertise or research to attain your goals? Also, find associate organisations or groups that can make your job easier.

7. **What kind of benefits would accrue to you?** Note down the benefits of achieving a particular goal. More the benefits, better the chances of you sticking to the goal. But be careful while setting the goals. Goals in one aspect of life must not come into conflict with those in another area.

8. **Have an action plan.** An action plan is a statement of a logical step-by-step approach leading to desired outcomes. Break down goals into sub-goals and minimize the opportunities for failures. Begin with some easy goals. Start by doing what is necessary, then what is possible, and suddenly you're doing the impossible.

9. **Motivate yourself and create passion.** Motivation is a powerful driving force in our lives. Goals motivate us and create a passion for our pursuits. Involve other people in the process and get feedback on a regular basis. Don't fear failures and encourage others. Stretch yourself to the limit; you will achieve more that way. Mario Andretti said: "Desire is the key to motivation, but it's determination and commitment to an unrelenting pursuit of your goal — a commitment to excellence — that will enable you to attain the success you seek."

10. **Be disciplined.** Discipline involves doing what needs to be done rather than what you would like to do. It involves taking responsibility for your behaviour and actions. Get focused and eliminate negative influences or factors. Identify time wasters and lead from the front. Get feedback from time to time; it will ensure that you are on the right track. If not, find the causes of failure and learn from them.

11. **Maintain flexibility.** Everything in this world is changing at a rapid pace. Be flexible and create an atmosphere that doesn't create fear or insecurity. Take people into confidence while making changes in structures, systems, strategies and technologies. A hard-line approach won't help your cause. Don't be too obsessive.

12. **Accomplish your goals and celebrate the same.** Evaluate your outcomes; they should be consistent with your identity and values. Before you embark on another mission, don't forget that you have accomplished something. It's time for celebration. Celebrations are important as they motivate you to take up bigger challenges in pursuit of excellence. Uncork the champagne now.

What does goal setting do for you?

- **It inspires you to do something.**
- **Helps you decide what you want to achieve.**
- **Increase your energy levels.**
- **Helps you remain in control of your life.**
- **Gives you a reason and value for your existence.**
- **Eliminates the irrelevant and unimportant.**
- **Builds self-confidence.**

It is a fact that individuals who have written goals become top achievers. According to a study done at Yale University in the early fifties, only three per cent of its students had written goals. Twenty years later, it was found that those three per cent were financially much better off than the remaining 97 per cent. This clearly demonstrates the power of goals.

Isn't it strange that people can organise parties, holidays or weddings but somehow fail to plan their lives? As a student you set goals to pass exams. Thereafter you plan to get a nice job and work on that goal. Marriage and children comes next. As we move into middle age, at around 35, complacency sets in and stagnation creeps into our lives. Complacency is the biggest enemy of motivation; to remain motivated, we need to set fresh goals. New goals will reactivate our energies and intelligence and bring back the passion and joy back into our lives. Goals are a great driving force and motivate us to achieve extraordinary things.

Why people don't set goals:

- **Ignorance of the importance of goals.**
- **Demotivated and laid-back attitude.**
- **Lack of desire to achieve excellence.**
- **Fear of failure.**
- **Fatalistic attitude.**
- **Lack of a burning desire.**

To keep ourselves motivated we should read biographies of successful people who have done wonders with their lives and those of others. Mother Teresa, Abraham Lincoln, Mahatma Gandhi, Nelson Mandela, Sardar Patel and Michael Jordan are some great individuals who fought against all odds and came out winners. They are the lighthouses of the world.

Qualities of successful people:

- **Desire to succeed.**
- **True vision.**
- **True purpose.**
- **Courage.**
- **Self-belief.**
- **Commitment.**
- **Ability to work hard and take responsibility.**
- **Character to withstand adversity.**

- **Persistence and perseverance.**
- **Resilience.**
- **Willingness to learn.**

Life is one indivisible whole; it is its wholeness that lends value to existence. We cannot put our life into compartments. Our life goals should be fair to all concerned since life is also a commitment, implying responsibility towards other citizens. It is all about trustworthiness, honesty, integrity, respect, responsibility, fairness, caring and an understanding that my life matters and so does that of every other creature.

ACTION SHEET

Identify what you want to accomplish this year and in the next three and five years and prioritize top three objectives.

GOALS	ACTION PLAN	TIME-PERIOD

WITHIN ONE YEAR:

Personal goals

1.

2.

3.

Professional goals

1.

2.

3.

WITHIN THREE YEARS:

Personal goals

1.

2.

3.

Professional goals

1.

2.

3.

WITHIN FIVE YEARS:

Personal goals

1.

2.

3.

Professional goals

1.

2.

3.

Don't forget to celebrate your accomplishments.

Daniel H. Burnham said: "Make no little plans, they have no magic to stir men's blood.... make big plans, aim high in hope and work." This quote has been attributed to Goethe: "The moment one definitely commits oneself, then providence moves too. All sort of things occur to help one that would never have otherwise occurred. A whole stream of events issues from the decision, raising in one's favour all manner of unforeseen incidents and meetings and material assistance which no man could have dreamed would have come his way. Whatever you can do or dream you can, begin it. Boldness has genius, power and magic in it. Begin it now."

❀ ❀ ❀

CHAPTER 3

RE-PROGRAM YOUR MIND FOR SUCCESS

We are what we repeatedly do. Excellence, then, is not an act, but a habit.

— Aristrotle

James Allen writes in *As a Man Thinketh*: "A man's mind may be likened to a garden, which may be intelligently cultivated or allowed to run wild; but whether cultivated or neglected, it must, and will, bring forth. If no useful seeds are put into it, then an abundance of useless weed seeds will fall therein, and will continue to produce their kind. Just as a gardener cultivates his plot, keeping it free from weeds, and growing the flowers and fruits which he requires, so may a man tend the garden of his mind, weeding out all the wrong, useless, and impure thoughts, and cultivating toward perfection the flowers and fruits of right, useful, and pure thoughts. By pursuing this process, a man sooner or later discovers that he is the master gardener of his soul, the director of his soul."

You get what you desire. If you seek heaven, you will get it. Look for hell and you're bound to get there. Everything is in the mind. Psychologically, our mind can be divided into two parts: the conscious and the sub-conscious. The conscious mind has analytical powers and can differentiate between good and bad or right and wrong. The sub-conscious is more like a dumping ground or a hard disk in a computer system. It stores only that data that we have entered into it.

We behave and act as per our mental programming. Think about how many times we make negative statements! We use the word 'no' tens of thousands of times during our lifetime. Even to our children, for every positive statement that we make, we utter 18 negative ones. According to research, 75 per cent of what we think is negative.

Negative statements we make on an everyday basis:

- **I have a weak memory.**
- **Nothing goes right for me.**
- **It is not correct.**
- **I just can't stop smoking.**
- **I am too shy.**
- **It's just not my day.**
- **I can never win.**
- **I don't have a creative mind.**
- **I can't do this.**
- **It's too big for me.**
- **I am not as talented.**
- **I am not that lucky.**
- **I am always short of time.**
- **I simply can't control my temper.**
- **I get agitated too easily.**
- **The workload is too much this week.**
- **It is another bad Saturday.**
- **This is not the age to learn computers.**
- **I am about to retire.**
- **My energy levels are low.**
- **This guy always beats me.**
- **God has been very unkind to me.**
- **I could not prepare much for the exams.**
- **It is not possible.**
- **Whatever I said is correct.**
- **I hate my job.**

- **I am not good at math.**
- **No one loves me.**
- **No one trusts me.**
- **I wish I were smarter and handsome.**
- **I wish I were born in a rich family.**
- **I wish I had gone to a better school.**

Do these words come automatically or are they the cumulative result of years of conditioning? Sometime back I was watching a practice hockey match. One of my young colleagues was playing in the centre-forward position. He scored three goals from the left flank but failed to convert any opportunity from the right. After the match, he conceded to me that he had always failed from the right flank and his opponents had capitalized on this particular weakness. When I asked him what stopped him from doing well on the right flank, he simply could not give a satisfactory reply. He had good technique, temperament and control but still struggled on the right flank. So why did he fail? He failed simply because he had a mental block that was activated each time he moved from the right.

Our perspective or programming determines how we view the world. It's the result of the directions that we give our mind. The sub-conscious mind does not differentiate between being right and left or right and wrong; it simply acts according to the directions it receives. When we use many negative words or statements every day, it's natural that our mental programming would tend to lean more on the negative side.

Negative words that we use to our children:

- **You are too clumsy.**
- **Who is responsible for this?**
- **You are just like your mother.**
- **You can't do a thing right.**

- **You make a mess of everything.**
- **You are always watching television.**
- **You are always in a playful mood.**
- **Be serious sometimes.**
- **Concentrate on your studies.**
- **You can never be like your brother.**
- **Why can't you think? You are not a small child.**
- **You are a liability.**
- **Do this or do that.**
- **Don't do this or that.**
- **It is bad or wrong.**

Do you think all these words leave the child unaffected? As a matter of fact, they penetrate the child's sub-conscious. We feel that we are helping our children through this type of training, but the end result is a pessimist. These 'can'ts' and negative directions are stored in the sub-conscious and influence all future action, habits and behaviour.

Garbage in, Garbage out

Success or failure is a matter of choice, not chance. Your choices directly reflect your conditioning process, which depends on the inputs or directions you give to your mind. Everything flows from this conditioning or programming. It is like the principles of a computer system. Its hard disk has software programs, which have been entered through a keyboard, an input device. A computer works on the GIGO — garbage in, garbage out — principle. The output you get depends on what you put in. A human mind too works on similar lines. If your mind is filled with filth, hatred and violence, it is a direct outcome of your mental programming.

Take for example how a terrorist works. A terrorist is trained in a certain philosophy or way of thinking and his mind is programmed to act accordingly. If you recollect the destruction of the World Trade Center in New York on 11 September 2001, you can get an idea of how such training works. It erased any kind of rational thinking from the terrorists' minds, substituting it with criminal rage, which is against every civic norm. Their minds are programmed in such a way that they simply work for a mission or a particular objective, unaffected by feelings of good and bad or right and wrong.

Belief, the biggest motivator

Our beliefs are the result of mental conditioning. Such beliefs are what enabled people like Tenzing Norgay or Bachendri Pal to scale peaks like Mount Everest. Unfortunately, they can also bring forth an Osama Bin Laden. Undoubtedly belief is the biggest motivator in life; people are even willing to die for it. Most wars have been fought for a belief. Alexander the Great believed that he could conquer the world and become the universal ruler. Napoleon too shared a similar vision. At one time the British had this belief that the sun would never set on their empire. A belief can have great creative or destructive power.

Our beliefs colour the way we look at things. Take for instance school and college text books. They describe the mutiny of 1857 as 'the first war of Indian Independence'; the British called it the 'sepoy mutiny'. We call Lala Lajpat Rai, Balgangadhar Tilak, Gopal Krishna Gokhale, Bhagat Singh and others freedom fighters; the British raj chose to call them traitors and enemies of state. Our mind treats people or events as it has been directed to do. Similarly our failures and successes are the direct result of our beliefs. Beliefs take people in the direction of their choices.

How attitudes work

Our attitudes, feelings, behaviour and actions flow from our beliefs. Our attitude influences the way we see people and things. We may feel good about certain things or people and see others in a negative light.

Habits influenced by attitude:

- Smoking and drinking.
- Getting up late every morning.
- Being witty.
- Being sarcastic.
- Coming late to work.
- Criticizing too much.
- Being unappreciative.
- Interrupting people while they are speaking (poor listening skills).
- Getting worked up about things.
- Making excuses all the time.
- Being disorganised at the office or at home.
- Giving way to emotional outbursts.
- Talking all the time.
- The friends we make and the people we avoid.
- Giving advice when not required.
- The kind of books or literature we read.
- Selfish behaviour.
- A greedy mentality.
- Being argumentative.
- Externally driven.
- Always reacting.
- Being arrogant.
- Taking an aggressive and offensive attitude.
- A fatalistic attitude.
- Being very sensitive and touchy.
- Feeling lonely.
- The music we listen to.

- Enjoying negative things like pornography.
- Looking down on others.
- Putting people down without any valid reason.
- Overeating and sleeping.

One can add to this list many other habits that people have at home or at the workplace. Why do people behave in such fashion? Habits are a matter of choice, and choices are a result of your mental programming. You control the choice before you make it, but once you have done it, it's the choice that controls you. A habit is undoubtedly a matter of choice.

How your feelings affects your behaviour

Our behaviour is the direct outcome of our feelings. Our behaviour passes through the filter of our feelings. If we feel good or positive about something, our behaviour towards it would be positive. Feel good and your productivity goes up, your relationships become sweeter and life becomes a lot smoother. Similarly, bad feelings culminate in soured relationships and lower productivity. Your physical state also depends on your feelings. You enjoy your food if you feel good; but if you feel bad, it tastes like ashes in your mouth.

Think of an everyday situation in the workplace. You might come across an individual who behaves with great courtesy and smiles one day while remaining aloof or unresponsive the next. Why do these paradoxical changes in behaviour take place? Believe me, everyone goes through the same experience; I too am no exception. Your behaviour is your action in the real world.

Sweep those old thoughts away

Management Guru Stephen Covey calls mental maps or

models 'Paradigms'. According to him, "it's the way we see the world — not in terms of our visual sense of sight, but in terms of perceiving, understanding and interpreting." A simple way of understanding paradigms is to see them as maps and not territories, he says.

Egyptian astronomer Ptolemy's paradigm was that the earth was at the centre of the universe and that the planets and the sun revolved around the earth. This thinking or hypothesis prevailed for a long time. It was only centuries later that Copernicus came up with the hypothesis that it was the sun that was at the centre of universe and not the earth. There was tremendous resistance to this new theory; people refused to accept this and ridiculed Copernicus for misguiding them. It was not easy for them to break away from the old thinking. Eventually, they accepted that Copernicus was right — in other words a 'paradigm shift'. Similarly, when Abraham Lincoln propounded that the government should be 'by the people, for the people, of the people', he broke away from the old paradigm of the middle ages that it was the divine right of kings to rule the people.

Japan rose from the ashes after the devastation of World War II through its unshakable resolve. In the words of a Japanese industrialist: "We are going to win and the industrialised West is going to lose, and there is nothing they can do about it." It is with such a mental model or roadmap that Japan became an economic powerhouse. Wrong mental maps can never lead one to the right path. The great navigator Christopher Columbus has been immortalized in history books as the man who discovered America. But it is also a fact that he had set out from Europe to find a sea route to India. If you rely on wrong maps, it is certain that you won't reach the right place or territory.

Most problems are due to wrong mental-maps

Most of the problems that we face are due to wrong mental maps or paradigms. It is here that re-programming the mind becomes of paramount importance. Some people try to use short cuts or quick-fixes to solve problems, or make cosmetic changes to tide them over hurdles. But the reality is that while these quick-fixes may work for some time, they are unsustainable in the long run. You can't achieve true success on a sustainable basis through old and obsolete practices.

However, it remains a fact that people love old practices or patterns and are averse to change. They feel safer sticking to the old paradigms or practices. These practices may be enough for present needs, but when things change they become obsolete. They don't work in the changed scenario, and slowly we begin to head for the wilderness. If we don't change even when that happens, that will be the end of us. Getting away from old ways of thinking is like breaking through the gravitational barrier; you require tremendous pull and energies.

Today's world is changing at a rapid pace and it is difficult to predict what may happen in the future. At such times, it becomes very difficult for an organisation to come up with correct long-term strategies. It would really become difficult to get a handle on the future. Only new and effective ways of thinking would enable us to face and overcome change, challenges, adversities and conflict. One needs to be focused, fast, flexible and friendly.

A physically challenged friend of mine is a very successful entrepreneur and operates from a wheelchair. One day, while I was sitting in his office, someone came for a business meeting with him. That person warmly greeted my friend and shook hands, but was irritated when my friend did not get up to greet him. He said: "I came here for a business meeting, but you don't have the decency to get up and receive your guests. I don't think I would like to have any business association with you or your firm." With a broad smile on his face, my friend listened to him patiently. The reaction of the guest was based on his existing paradigm, through which he understood and interpreted the situation. Little did he realize that the reality was totally different from what he had perceived. Soon my friend said: "I do understand your dilemma and respect your viewpoint. But it's not out of disrespect that I didn't get up. God has taken away my limbs and I operate from a wheelchair. I hope you understand. Hopefully we can now begin our meeting." At that very moment, the paradigm of the business client changed. He felt embarrassed and apologized for his words. Sometimes we feel we are right about something when the reality is altogether different. It's necessary that we also see things from the other person's angle too. That's real empathy.

Most of the problems that we face or confront — whether it is in the family, organisations or the community — are not due to bad people. They have their origin in bad systems. But the question is, who devises these systems? Only people are programmers, everything else is a program. If the people who devise the systems are hypocrites, what kind of systems would they design? Are they not living with old, obsolete and outdated paradigms? The need again is to re-program yourself into a new way of thinking. It is also necessary to look at things or the world around us with a changed mindset or with a new frame of reference.

Norman Vincent Peale's books on positive thinking have influenced millions of people around the world. Peale dealt with a whole range of subjects — thinking, attitude, feelings, emotions, mental makeup. According to him, we need to make subtle changes in our thinking process, which would lead to dynamic results. Earlier, I dealt with negative thinking and habits that create roadblocks on our way to happiness and prosperity. It's good to get rid of bad habits and attitudes, but if they are not replaced by good ones, the negative habits tend to get back into our sub-conscious in no time. Our minds get used to such thinking patterns over time so it won't be easy to erase old habits unless there are new and positive ones to replace them.

If you want to bring about that change in your thinking, think positively. Only you can bring about dynamic change in your life. You would be making a mistake if you wait for an outside agent or motivator since only you know best what you are; don't expect anyone else to know you better than yourself.

Follow these steps to a new life:

1. **Decide about your needs and wants:** Look for the reasons that are preventing you from having fulfilling them. Ask yourself whether you are ready to make the mental changes necessary to get rid of old and obsolete thinking patterns that are hindering your way to progress and prosperity.

2. **Think of the consequences:** Would you rather maintain the status quo and suffer the pain that it entails? What benefits would you derive if you make these changes now?

3. **Eliminate the old and obsolete thinking patterns:** These are like the old junk furniture in your house that cannot be put to the use they were intended for and have lost their utility.

4. **Substitute the old patterns with new patterns immediately:** The moment you change the old patterns that are in your mind, replace them with new ones immediately. If you fail to make the substitution, the old patterns will creep back in no time and things will get back to what they were earlier.

5. **Remind yourself about the new patterns on an everyday basis:** Our sub-conscious has to be reminded repeatedly about the new changes so that the old patterns are erased from the hard disk of our minds. Let new thinking create new habits; stick to them and use them on an everyday basis. Talk to yourself positively many times a day so that the new thinking or pattern is firmly imprinted on your mind.

   Some positive things to think about:

   - **I am good at math.**
   - **I have a good memory.**
   - **I can take responsibility.**
   - **I'll do the things I want to do.**
   - **I am capable.**

6. **Validate new patterns over a time period:** Make a check-list to see whether the new pattern is working smoothly and whether it has brought the desired changes in your beliefs, attitudes, feelings and actions.

I believe that God has designed and equipped human brains to be successful. Why then do we fail to make use of this design and equipment? It is because we use the wrong programming to operate them. We program ourselves to fail and then blame the whole world. We may have the best of ships and the most favourable of winds, but if we don't know our destination, we will drift forever aimlessly. There is only one way of being a success and that is by re-programming your minds to meet the change, challenges and adversity in this ever-changing and unpredictable world.

There is an old saying: "The wise man changes his mind sometimes; the fool never."

ACTION SHEET

Write down the old habits that are hindering your progress:

1.

2.

3.

What new habits do I need to replace the old ones?

1.

2.

3.

Henry Ford said: "Ideas are of themselves extraordinarily valuable, but an idea is just an idea. Almost anyone can think up an idea. The thing that counts is developing it into a practical product."

CHAPTER 4

COMMUNICATE EFFECTIVELY

Communication is the largest single factor determining what kinds of relationships we have with others and what happens to us in the world around us.

— Virginia Satir

In 1973, Henry Mintzberg conducted a study on the nature of managerial work in various organisations. He found that a manager spent 75 per cent of his work time communicating with others. Of this, six per cent of the time was spent on the telephone, 10 per cent on unscheduled meetings and 59 per cent on scheduled meetings. This of course did not include the time spent on written communication.

Communication is a process through which people exchange and share ideas and thoughts through symbolic messages. It is the lifeblood of any family, organisation or community and a key factor in building relationships. Effective communication means creating understanding in the minds of others around you; its effectiveness depends on the way the message is transmitted and received. Better communication inevitably leads to improved productivity, a better understanding of human relationships and ultimate success.

Since, as we noted earlier, people in organisations spend over 75 per cent of their time communicating with each other, it comes as no surprise that poor communication is at the root of a large number of organisational problems. Effective communication is an essential component of organisational success.

In the mid-eighties, Hallmark was one of the biggest greeting card makers in the world. Hallmark took pride in the fact that it never compromised on quality and creativity. But by 1991, it was facing a peculiar problem. The company was taking about 18 months to produce a new card from concept to the final product stage. It was far too long: competitors were taking far less time to come out with newer and attractive products, eating into Hallmark's marketshare.

When the management looked into why it was taking so long, it unearthed that there was very little communication among the various departments that dealt with the development of a new product. Some of the departments were in fact located far away and there was virtually no communication among them. The company then lost no time in relocating these departments into the same building so that employees could communicate and share their ideas in meetings and brainstorming sessions. It worked wonders: the time needed to bring out a new product dropped from 18 months to around eight months. Better inter-personal communication had led to improved productivity.

It shouldn't surprise anybody that verbal communication accounts for approximately 10 per cent of total communication. Most communication takes place through body language, and various other channels — radio, television, newspapers, e-mail, telephone, signboards, letters, bulletin boards etc.

Non-verbal communication can be broadly divided into following parts:

1. **Visual or body language:** This includes facial expressions, eye movements, body posture, gestures and limb movements. The face is the biggest part of this type of communication and it is capable of expressing a gamut of emotions. Body posture can indicate self-confidence, fear, aggression, guilt, or anxiety. A good posture is associated with confidence and enthusiasm. It also indicates the degree of tension or relaxation. Gestures too are important, .but they mean different things in different cultures. They can easily be misinterpreted.

2. **Tactile:** This involves the use of touch to convey something, as in a handshake, a pat on the back, an arm around the shoulder, a kiss, or a hug.

3. **Vocal:** Different emotions or feelings can be conveyed using various tones. You can say 'no' in many ways — to express mild doubt, terror or force, amazement, resentment, bitterness and anger etc.

4. **Use of time:** Time can be used as an indication of our status and power and define relationships with others. Think how a subordinate or superior would view your respect or disrespect for time.

The father of psychoanalysis Sigmund Freud said: "No mortal can keep a secret. If his lips are silent he chatters with his fingertips; betrayal oozes out of him from every pore."

Ram Prasad was a union leader in an organisation. He was a good worker but every time he entered his manager's room, there were heated arguments between the two. Ram Prasad was unable to understand why this happened only with the manager; he had no problems with his other co-workers. He discussed the matter with his co-workers, who decided they should enact a scene between him and the manager to get to the root of the problem. One of the co-workers played the role of the manager and waited for Ram Prasad in his room. Before entering the room, Ram Prasad rolled up his sleeves and then entered with his hands on his hips — a body posture that conveyed aggression. Ram Prasad was unaware of his body language and the message it was conveying to his manager. His body conveyed something that his speech did not; there was no congruence between his words and his body posture.

Indian Prime Minister Atal Bihari Vajpayee, former US President Bill Clinton or Microsoft Chairman Bill Gates keep their audience in thrall when they speak. Bollywood legends Amitabh Bachchan, Raj Kumar and Dilip Kumar owed their success largely to their effective dialogue delivery, which mesmerized the audience and kept them spell-bound. Abraham Lincoln, John F. Kennedy and Winston Churchill too were great communicators. How could they communicate so well and keep people mesmerized? The main reason why they could was because there was a strong congruence between their body language and their words.

Why do school children wear uniforms? By wearing them they communicate unity, oneness and equity. How do we recognize a porter at a railway station or airline personnel at an airport? From their uniforms. Uniforms are a powerful communicator, conveying a strong message.

Similarly your body language and facial expressions send clear signals about your moods. Invariably, when we come out of a theatre after seeing a movie, we tend to appreciate or criticize the performance of actors/actresses or the movie itself. We easily recollect scenes that convey powerful expressions. Although movies, television or the print media involve only one-way communication, they are an important part of life.

Building trust and relationships through communication

In everyday life we communicate at various levels. Intrapersonal communication is within oneself whereas interpersonal communication is with other people in the family, organisation and community. At the managerial level, communication is inter- or intra-departmental or organisational. Effective communication is all about building and maintaining good relationships. And trust is at the core of every relationship. Whether it is between a husband and his wife, a buyer and a seller, a student and his teacher, an employer and the employee or a father and his son. Without trust there can't be a relationship. Organisations can't hope for long-term success unless they build trust among their clients and customers. And they can't do this unless they have leaders who create and maintain trust at all levels.

What is trust? Trust is a cement or glue that binds relationships. Trustworthiness is at the core of ethical values. At a personal level, if we lack character and have dubious integrity, would we be trustworthy? Trustworthiness implies honesty, sincerity, loyalty, integrity, empathy, compassion and judiciousness. Honesty is the biggest fundamental value. We always honour and admire people who are truthful and righteous. According to Henry L. Stimson, "The chief lesson I have learned in a long life is that the only way to make a man trustworthy is to trust him; and the surest way to make him untrustworthy is to distrust him and show your mistrust."

Integrity is the most important factor in trust. It implies reliability, dependability, predictability, caring and mutual respect and understanding. Integrity is the keystone that guarantees self-esteem, self-confidence, inner peace and great success.

Galford and Drapeau have identified three types of trust within organisations — strategic, organisational and personal. They maintain that strategic trust is the faith people have in their organisation's ability to do things right, in terms of its goals and strategies. Organisational trust is their faith in the company's processes and decision-making. And personal trust is the employees' confidence in the leader as an individual.

Trust works wonders at the managerial level, empowering people and helping release blocked energies and creativity. Trust needs two conditions: character and integrity, and proficiency or competence. An individual has to fulfill each condition before he can earn trust. Let me illustrate. You have a very important and confidential assignment dealing with the company's future marketing strategies. Now you want this assignment to be done by your employees. If your subordinate is competent but short on integrity, would you hand over the assignment to him? No way. On the other hand, if he is a man of integrity but not very competent, would you trust him for this assignment? Obviously your reply would be no.

Building trust at a personal level begins with the process of connecting with someone and ending with a commitment to act in concert with that person to achieve a goal. People feel less stressed when they are trusted and are able to take on the responsibility. Trust also enables people to communicate with clarity and confidence and resolve problems, no matter what they are. Lack of trust in relationships leads to stress, bitterness, irritation, suspicion, isolation, anger, disappointment, conflict, distrust and poor productivity. Personal and professional success depends largely on how we conduct ourselves.

Sometimes you don't need big words or speeches to communicate what is important. One can easily convey a big message through one's acts. I recollect an incident involving Ishwarchandra Vidyasagar. Vidyasagar was a very learned person, and there are many anecdotes about his humility, sacrifice and love for justice.

Once a young man arrived at Howrah railway station and started looking for a porter to carry his luggage. But there was no porter around and the young man stood there helplessly, wondering what to do. Noticing his predicament, a simple-looking person asked him where he wanted to go. When the young man mentioned the name of a nearby college where he had come to study, the simple-looking person promptly picked up the luggage and took the student there. When the young man offered him some money, the man refused and said one should try to do one's own work and not depend on others for such small jobs. The next day the young man was shocked to see that the man who had carried his luggage was none other than the principal of the college! Aghast, he fell at the feet of the man, who was none other than Vidyasagar. The young man learnt a valuable lesson that day.

Why empathy, mutual respect and understanding are important

In the early twentieth century, US steel baron Andrew Carnegie appointed Charles Schwab president of his company, making him one of the few million dollar-earning executives at the time. Schwab had joined the steel company in 1879 as a labourer and rose quickly to the top. Now the moot question was: why did Carnegie pay him so much? Was he a steel genius? Was no one else better than him at that time? Schwab coolly replied to this question: "I consider my ability to arouse enthusiasm among my people... the greatest asset I possess, and the way to develop the best that it is in a person is by appreciation and encouragement." According to him, "there is nothing else that so kills the ambitions of a person as criticism from superiors. I never criticize anyone. I believe in giving a person incentive to work. So I am anxious to praise but loath to find fault. If I like anything, I am hearty in my approbation and lavish in my praise."

Knowledge comprises only 12 per cent of effective management strategy; 88 per cent involves dealing appropriately with people.

After he came back to India from South Africa in the early part of the twentieth century, Mahatma Gandhi was passing through a village with his wife Kasturba when he noticed an elderly woman in a very dirty sari sitting outside her hut. He asked Kasturba to speak to the woman on the importance of wearing clean clothes. It was not a crime to be poor, said Gandhi, but one should be clean. After speaking to the old woman, Kasturba reported back to Gandhi that the lady had only one pair of clothes and if she washed that what would she wear? Such abject poverty shook Gandhi. That day he vowed to wear only a loincloth until his fellow countrymen could afford two pairs of simple and reasonable clothes. Empathy and sacrifice are the hallmark of great men. Probably that is why a Gandhi is not born every day.

When you treat people with respect, empathy and understanding, you befriend them. Fine relationships always leads to a better life.

Smile, it doesn't cost a thing

A few months back, I had gone to a department store to buy a few things. While I was talking to a salesperson, I noticed a cute little girl on a wheelchair with her parents. As she came closer, I noticed that she had no legs at all. When I asked the parents how this came to be, they said she had lost them in an accident. I felt sad for her, and my face became grim when I thought about the torture the little girl was going through. But to my surprise the little girl was full of energy and raring to go. My sadness evaporated when I saw her cute smile and I felt love and warmth that I had not felt for years. A smile is the best gift you can give some one. It costs you nothing. The giver doesn't get poorer but the receiver surely gets richer.

The power of influencing people

According to a survey of Human Resources Directors from Fortune 1000 firms, the top 10 skills managers need for organisational success are: interpersonal skills, listening, persuasion and motivating, presentation, small group communication, advising, interviewing, conflict management, writing and reading.

Influencing skills have become far more important these days. The more we need cooperation, consent, agreement and empathy, the more important inter-personal influencing skills become. We may also call it the power of persuasion. Influencing is not like trying to sell something — whether it's an idea, model or hypothesis. It is our ability to present our viewpoint and ideas with greater clarity, logic and confidence. Many a time, we reject an idea, services, products or suggestions because we have negative feelings and attitudes at the time. Influencing also means understanding people and their viewpoints and adding value to their perspectives.

Remembering people's names is one way of influencing people. People love their identities and are attached to their names. American President Franklin D. Roosevelt was a very busy person but had the very good habit of remembering names. He used to shock people by addressing them by their names, gaining a lot of goodwill that way. You can apply this technique to influence people too. If someone introduces himself to you, ask him to repeat his name or ask him how it's spelt so that you can retain it permanently in your memory.

Good influencing skills does not mean being hypocritical or dishonest. Truthfulness and honesty form the core of any relationship. Being false might work for a while but you can't keep it up in the long run. People will see through you sooner or later.

Hello, are you listening?

Andre Gide once began his lecture by saying: "All this has been said before, but since nobody listened, it must be said again." Listening is the most important part of the communication process. Unfortunately everyone talks about it, but no one does a thing about it. Listening helps us understand other people's thinking, feelings and behaviour. It enables us to concentrate on what the other person is saying. It creates empathy when we are able to understand the other person's viewpoint.

Situations and behaviour to avoid:

- **Someone is speaking to you but you are busy with the phone and several other things.**
- **You hear only what you want to hear, and avoid listening to negative, unpleasant and critical words.**
- **You jump to conclusions before the other person has finished speaking.**

- **You are speaking but your body language is saying something else. There is no congruence.**
- **You interrupt others frequently, thus breaking the communication.**
- **You use terrible, insulting, humiliating and embarrassing words when you talk.**

What most people don't realize that it's the listener who controls the communication and not the speaker. The next time you listen to another person, try to understand the feelings behind the words. They may range from complimentary, complaining, suggestive, defensive, cooperative or aggressive. If possible try to earmark a day for listening only and see the difference in people's attitude towards you.

How to be a good listener:

- **Look for areas of common interest.**
- **Maintain good eye contact.**
- **Be warm to the speaker.**
- **Take notes.**
- **Keep an open mind.**
- **Don't interrupt the flow.**
- **Be actively responsive.**
- **Resist distractions.**
- **Have patience.**
- **Show empathy with the speaker.**
- **Assist and encourage the speaker.**
- **Avoid jumping to conclusions.**
- **Avoid making unpleasant and critical comments.**
- **Make the speaker feel important.**
- **Let the other person do most of the talking.**

As a speaker in seminars, I meet a lot of people. Sometime back I met a friend who was working in a multinational company as vice-president, marketing. He had attended my seminars and the meeting began on a warm note. After exchanging pleasantries, I asked him about his experiences as a marketing executive and how he dealt with people and pressures. Thereafter I simply listened to him for more than an hour, doing nothing but nod once in a while. He talked at length about his student life, training, love and marriage and many other things. Finally, when we got up to leave, he had a glow on his face and profusely thanked me for a very healthy and useful conversation although I had not spoken a single word! Before leaving, he requested me to conduct a few more seminars for his firm, since they would be very useful to his employees.

According to Dr. Harrell T. Allen, "Listening is hard work. It requires increased energy, your blood circulates faster and your temperature goes up."

Management guru Stephen Covey said: "Seek first to understand, then to be understood... when we listen with the intent to reply, we begin true communication and relationship-building. When others feel understood first, they feel affirmed and valued, defences are lowered, and opportunities to speak openly and to be understood come much more naturally and easily. Seeking to understand takes kindness; seeking to be understood takes courage. Effectiveness lies in balancing the two."

Pay attention to the speaker and listen attentively. You will add immense value to him. Isn't winning friends easy?

Criticize, but in a constructive way

You had your house refurbished and are feeling good about it. You think the house and the furnishings are looking gorgeous when someone comes in and says: "It looks fine but green would have been better than pink. And had you chosen period furniture, things would have been different." You feel disgusted and annoyed with this visitor. People make critical comments without giving a thought to the other person's feelings; it's a powerful de-motivator and deflator.

Criticism can be either constructive or destructive. Insulting a physically challenged person because of his disability really hurts. Telling a person rudely that he is 10 minutes late will definitely create bad feelings because you haven't asked him the reasons for being late. By using a soft voice and non-threatening body language, along with a focus on suggestions rather than orders, you will find that people will become more receptive to you.

How to criticize constructively:

- **Never humiliate the other person.**
- **Invite the person's attention to his mistake indirectly.**
- **Be specific while criticizing.**
- **Criticize the mistakes, not the person.**
- **Explain the benefits of corrections.**
- **Make the mistake easy to correct.**
- **Give the person breathing space to understand the mistakes.**
- **Offer the other person an opportunity to explain.**
- **See things from the other person's perspective.**
- **Keep personal matters aside.**
- **Don't be an egomaniac while criticizing.**
- **Don't question the intentions of the person you're criticizing.**
- **Don't tarnish the reputation of the person you're criticizing.**
- **Respect the other person's ideas and desires.**
- **Don't enter into arguments.**
- **Begin and close the conversation with a smile.**

One of my subordinates had prepared a difficult report,

which was not up to the mark. I told him: "This report is pretty fine but I'm sure you can do things in a much better way." This way I could tell him he could improve on it without hurting his feelings. "Indeed," he said, "this report could have been better, had I concentrated more." This is constructive criticism, which deals with the content and not the intent.

Buddhist scriptures also speak eloquently about the right communication process. Right Speech is the third jewel in Gautama Buddha's Eight-Fold Path. Buddha described Right Speech as "abstaining from lies, divisive speeches, abusive speeches and idle chatter."

Buddha's five conditions for right speech:

- **Do I speak at the right time?**
- **Do I speak the facts?**
- **Do I speak harshly or gently?**
- **Do I use profitable words or not?**
- **Do I speak with a kind heart, without malice?**

When we look at modern theories of communication and inter-personal behaviour, we find that they are no different from ancient concepts.

Appreciation is the key

While preparing for a seminar on "Inter-personal skills and how to maximize human potential", I came upon an interesting observation. It stated that appreciation and praise are far more powerful motivators than money or anything else. They help us become more receptive and we concentrate on things that we can appreciate. There are many things — people, interactions and experiences — that deserve appreciation or praise.

Are you an appreciative person?

- **Do you appreciate food cooked by your spouse?**
- **Do you appreciate your wife's new set of jewels?**
- **Do you appreciate the sincere efforts of your friends towards a certain cause?**
- **Do you appreciate the good marks your child got in the exam?**
- **Do you take note of the good work done by your secretary?**
- **Do you compliment your subordinate for taking initiative?**
- **Do you appreciate someone's beautiful smile?**
- **Do you realize that praise is a powerful motivator?**
- **Do you know that sincere praise leads to better relationships and productivity?**

My daughter had won a few contests being held by a local FM Radio station and had been asked to collect her prizes at the station. When I took her to the station, many people were waiting to receive their prizes. The lady at the reception had a harried look as she checked and confirmed names, gave prizes and attended to telephone calls in between. When I approached her, she asked in a very abrupt and officious tone to wait for a few minutes. Finally, when my daughter was given the prizes, I told that lady: "Your job must be very taxing, attending to an unending stream of calls and clients. But you seem to be doing pretty fine. Had I been in your place, I don't think I could have done any better." My words worked wonders for the lady. Her face broke out into a broad smile and she attended to us with sincerity, thanking me for the appreciation and understanding.

How to use appreciation to motivate people:

- **Listen more, talk less.**
- **Use first names while addressing people.**

- **Be polite and respectful to others.**
- **Ask politely instead of giving orders.**
- **Be generous and encouraging.**
- **Give credit wherever it is due.**
- **Don't make sarcastic comments.**
- **Laugh with the people you work with.**
- **Keep your people informed.**
- **Be flexible and friendly.**
- **Smile a lot.**
- **Admit your mistakes first before pointing out others' shortcomings.**

Sometime ago, I was in Delhi to conduct a seminar on leadership, and my clients had chosen a state-owned hotel as the venue. When I reached the hotel an hour before the appointed time to check if everything was in place and there was no last-minute hitch, I was shocked. The seminar hall was virtually stinking; it had not been cleaned after an overnight party. I rushed to the reception and spoke to the person on the front desk. To my dismay, I was informed that it was not his job to get the room cleaned. I was running out of time, and it looked impossible to begin the session on time. My hosts were also upset and apologetic.

Instead of losing my temper, I decided to take a different approach with the lobby manager. I began by appreciating the hotel, its courteous people and the neat surroundings. The lobby manager was very pleased with what I said; he took great pride in being the lobby manager of this reputed hotel. I then told him that I was here to conduct a seminar for my clients and it would be nice of him if he could see the final arrangements in the seminar hall. When he accompanied me to the hall, he was shocked to see the mess. He apologized profusely and begged me for fifteen minutes to put the hall in order.

Abraham Lincoln said: "If you want to win a man to your cause, first convince him that you are his real friend."

Barriers to communication

To make our communication more effective, we must overcome certain barriers. These barriers can be broadly classified into the following categories:

Sender-related barriers:

- Poor communication skills.
- Interpersonal sensitivity.
- Different perceptions and paradigms.
- Low credibility of the sender.
- Inappropriate and unintelligible language.
- Different values and attitude.
- Poorly expressed contents.

Situation-related barriers:

- Use of jargon.
- Insufficient time.
- Distance and climate.
- Physical distractions.
- Mechanical failures.

Receiver-related barriers:

- Selective attention.
- Poor listening and instant interpretation.
- Tendency to be judgmental.
- Predisposition to jump to conclusions.
- Improper feedback.
- Different perceptions and paradigms.
- Inappropriate language.
- Different values and attitude.

Other barriers:

- Heightened emotions.
- Status effect.
- Vague presumptions.
- Multiple meanings.
- Information overload.
- Cultural differences.

How to communicate better:

- Be polite and courteous.
- Keep the message simple and short.
- Ensure clarity of thought.
- Avoid technical jargon.
- Involve people in the communication process.
- Keep the receiver in mind.
- Give and get feedback on a continuous basis.
- Listen carefully and be empathetic.
- Use direct and indirect channels of communication.

Effective way of sending messages:

- Decide what exactly you want to say.
- Attract the other person's attention.
- Use language that's understood by the receiver.
- Ensure congruence between your verbal and non-verbal communication.
- Get feedback.
- Find out why you're not getting the response you want.

Words you can avoid:

No	Can't
Impossible	Why
What	Wait
Should've	How
But	

Six most important words:

- **I admit I made a mistake.**
- **I am proud of you.**
- **What is your opinion?**
- **If you please.**
- **Thank you.**
- **We.**

Least important word:

- **I**

Ideal space zones in communication

How far apart should we be when we're talking to another person? Anthropologist Edward T. Hall, a pioneer in the study of man's spatial needs, says there are four zones that people consciously or unconsciously use during the course of their interaction.

Intimate Zone (15 cm to 46 cm): We allow people who are very close to us — close friends, lovers, spouses and children — into this zone. We feel threatened and embarrassed if an unknown person tries to enter this zone. However there are exceptions, that is, when we travel by train or stand in a queue. At such times, despite being so near physically, we avoid eye contact.

Personal Zone (46 cm to 1.2 m): A zone of comfort. We maintain this distance during social gatherings, while speaking to people.

Social Zone (1.2 m to 3.6 m): We keep this distance with strangers or people who we don't know.

Public Zone (over 3.6 m): This distance is maintained when large groups of people are addressed.

Essentials in inter-personal communication:

- **Treat people with courtesy and respect.**
- **Take genuine interest in people.**
- **Encourage others to speak.**
- **Make people feel important.**
- **Respect other people's opinion.**
- **Show empathy.**
- **Accepting mistakes without shame or guilt.**
- **Avoid arguments.**
- **Never criticize without a valid reason.**
- **Never tarnish other people's reputations.**
- **Avoid making embarrassing comments.**
- **Never be personal while criticizing.**
- **Begin and end your conversation with a smile.**

The essence of every successful communication lies in its simplicity. Honesty and simplicity in spoken and written communication is an effective tool to win friends and influence people. Don't you agree?

ACTION SHEET

Write down your good communication skills:

1.

2.

3.

4.

5.

Do you have these qualities?

- Empathy.

- Good listening skills.
- Good influencing skills.
- The power of making positive criticism.
- Appreciating things when they are well done.

CHAPTER 5

LEADERSHIP: WHAT MAKES A GOOD LEADER?

The height by great men reached and kept
Were not attained by sudden flight,
But they while their companions' slept,
Were toiling upward in the night.

— Longfellow

In 1981, Jack Welch took over as the youngest chairman of General Electric (GE). GE was passing through a tough time at the time and the company needed someone who could bring about sweeping changes to restore it to its past glory. The company was burdened with a heavy structure, with multiple layers of hierarchy. Welch observed that the heavy structure was obstructing and delaying the decision-making process; the bureaucratic style of functioning was evident in almost every department. Welch was convinced that eliminating several layers at one go would result in better 'compliance and communication' and help delegate power to the middle and lower level of management.

Welch did exactly that. He reduced the top management layer by almost half. He also took unpleasant decisions like reducing corporate staff by almost 40% and making huge cuts in the workforce. These drastic measures had an adverse impact on morale and there was a sharp polarization among the employees. Things came to such a pass that the labour unions in GE came up with a slogan: "GE has a disease called Welch-ese". But notwithstanding his detractors, Welch had a lot of admirers who appreciated the bold steps he had taken. Jack Welch was out to make GE number one in every business it was in. He faced challenges with courage, determination and discipline, and brought to GE a vision and passion to change.

It wasn't long before his strategies turned the company's fortunes around; GE and Jack Welch became synonymous. Welch is now regarded as an icon in effective organisational leadership. He said: "If you pick the right people and give them the opportunity to spread their wings — and put compensation as a carrier behind it — you almost don't have to manage them."

The word leadership brings different images to mind — of people like Mahatma Gandhi, Abraham Lincoln, Martin Luther King, Nelson Mandela and many others. Some people see leadership as charisma, while others relate it to power. In his survey of leadership theories and research, Ralph M. Stogdill said: "There are almost as many different definitions of leadership as there are persons who have attempted to define the concept." To put it simply, leadership is the process of directing and influencing people to get the assigned job accomplished effectively within a time frame. If there are leaders, there's got to be followers. Leadership must have a tinge of power or authority to enable a leader to influence people and make them comply with his directions. But the most valued part of any kind of leadership — whether it is in the family, organisation, community or country — is moral and ethical.

Before the 1980s, good leadership was usually synonymous with assertive decision-making. Leaders were appreciated for their courage and risk-taking abilities while coming up with future strategies. However, times have changed. Today, leaders have to look beyond day-to-day operations and taking tough decisions. They are expected to be social scientists who have mastered the art of motivation, and possess the ability to understand people and tap into their resourcefulness and innate capacities.

Long before anyone came up leadership theories, dictatorial chieftains and kings ruled everything. They in turn were conquered by others who had better leadership skills. In his time, Alexander the Great was the epitome of leadership. In addition to demonstrating his greatness and decisiveness through his own accomplishments, he brought the weaknesses of others to light.

Alexander died at the age of 33 in 323 BC. He led an incredible campaign that took him as far as India before he died on his way home. Most historians accept the fact that he was a very charismatic leader; he set lofty goals for himself and showed an exemplary commitment to them. His teacher was none other than the Greek philosopher Aristotle, and it has been speculated that he inspired Alexander into exploring the geographic limits of the world. Alexander dared to take the land route to India, which was considered highly unconventional in those days. He certainly fits the description of a transformational leader.

Visionary leaders embody great values and principles that become the guideposts for humanity, like the USA's Thomas Jefferson and his Declaration of Independence. Such leaders intuitively draw on their reserves of wisdom and apply it to meet the particular needs of the time.

An ideal leadership must be based on principles and deal with all aspects of life — the body, heart, mind and spirit

— effectively. Noted ethicist Michael Josephson: "We don't learn ethics from people who sermonize or moralize or try to preach to us about ethics; we learn ethics from the people whom we admire and respect, who have power over us. They're the real teachers of ethics... it's important to reinforce ideals, if they are sincere. It is very important for leaders and role models, whether they be sports figures or politicians, to make positive statements of ethics, if they're not hypocritical." In a recent survey by the Industrial Society, 82 per cent of UK professionals claimed that they would not work for an organisation whose values they did not believe in. Over half (59 per cent) said they had chosen the company they worked for because they believed in what it did or stood for, and almost everyone (99 per cent) said they cared whether the organisation they worked for acted responsibly or not.

It is worth noting that the leadership model of the industrial age was based on management or control. But in today's knowledge era, leadership is based on release — that is, unleashing potential and releasing the blocked energies. A knowledge-based leadership concentrates on building teams and creating good relationships. The leaders lead by example, trust, and empowerment: A spirit of service guides them. In the absence of these factors the workplace will become dysfunctional.

Management guru Stephen Covey quotes Mahatma Gandhi on the subject of an unconventional way of leading, servant leadership: "Gandhi had many personal struggles with his impatience and anger, but he overcame them with a vision of the independence of India which was far greater than his ego. He brought England to its knees and liberated India. He was never elected. He didn't have formal authority."

Today's business world is littered with the debris of corporate scams and frauds; morals and ethics have taken a back seat in many business houses. Mere rules cannot change this situation; the solution lies in cultivating integrity and a commitment to values. However, most companies consider enhancing the financial assets of its owners as their main aim. They do not usually examine the entire gamut of activities within the organisation, like the work culture and the quality of relationships. The solution lies in a personal value system that is in harmony with true principles. Anything else would just be a stop-gap arrangement and is not sustainable in the long run.

The world is changing rapidly and the only way to remain competitive in a market place is to properly nurture and develop leaders and leadership at all levels of organisation. It will definitely involve more than just producing people with a set of well-polished skills and competencies. Good leadership is also about having the vision to serve organisational objectives and people. Good leaders care about the individuals they lead; they are committed to serving their followers and their organisations for the good of all. In the true sense, leadership is the art of energizing and mobilizing people at all levels. Here are some qualities of an ideal leadership:

1. Vision and Focus

According to Webster's dictionary, vision is "the ability to perceive something not actually visible, as through mental acuteness and keen foresight". A vision is a coherent and powerful statement of what the organisation can and should become within a certain time-frame. If you look at the vision statement of any good organisation, you will realize that it's based on certain fundamentals.

Fundamentals of a vision statement:

- **It must present a holistic picture, which incorporates organisational goals, strategies and action plans.**
- **It should be a powerful statement that motivates people and ensures commitment to optimize performance at all levels.**
- **It must provide a roadmap to look into the future and say what the organisation could become and what can be realistically achieved.**
- **It must define the value system and aspirations of all stakeholders, providing a firm foundation on which the organisation works.**

The vision must be shared by most employees within the organisation. The purpose of vision statements is to stimulate action and achieve results, not just to have a few juicy platitudes on the walls. It should ideally become an integral part of the organisation's culture. GE's Jack Welch used every public and corporate opportunity, in speeches, meetings, articles, and interviews, to drive his message home. Vision necessarily has to be backed by action. Dhirubhai Ambani of the Reliance group said: "I keep revising my vision. Only when you dream it you can do it."

In the sixties, the Soviets stunned the world by sending the first person into space. On 12 April 1961, cosmonaut Yuri Gagarin orbited the earth in his Vostok spacecraft and landed safely. Gagarin's flight took place a month before American astronaut Alan Shepard's sub-orbital flight, and 10 months before astronaut John Glenn became the first American to orbit the earth. The USA was quick to respond to the Soviet challenge. On 25 May 1961, President John F. Kennedy announced the goal of landing a man on the moon. When the USA embarked on the space race with the Soviet Union, it was backed by a vision as well as rivalry with the Soviet Union. Kennedy's vision was to put a man on the moon before the end of the decade, and also before the Soviet Union did it.

After several manned missions to test the feasibility of landing a man on the moon, Apollo 11 — with Neil Armstrong, Edwin Aldrin, and Collins as crew — was launched. Apollo 11 lifted off on 16 July 1969 at 9:32 a.m. eastern daylight time. Four days later, Neil Armstrong landed the lunar module Eagle in the Sea of Tranquillity and for the first time man set foot on the moon. A dream had come true for humankind.

What vision and focus does for us:

- **Inspire us to be creative.**
- **Create energy and inspire action**
- **Help realize latent possibilities.**
- **Plan to meet future challenges.**
- **Activate us to achieve our goals.**
- **Provide us with a clear direction and establish the desired outcome.**
- **Help us look at possibilities, not impossibilities.**
- **Create responsibility.**
- **Provide a view of the future.**

A vision differs from, but complements, the mission and philosophy of any individual, organisation or country. A mission statement speaks about the basic purpose of an organisation, defines its relationships with other organisations and its constituents and sets general objectives. The philosophy of an organisation consists of the values that guide organisational behaviour, defines the character of relationships with other stakeholders, and sets the style and culture of the organisation. Vision builds on these statements and describes the organisational size, shape, and texture. It sets the tone for specific organisational goals and objectives and envisages an action plan to achieve them. The mission and philosophy of an organisation are timeless whereas vision expresses its goals at a particular time. True leadership uses vision, mission and philosophy to enable the organisation to achieve set goals and objectives.

What would our lives be if we didn't have a vision? The success of any individual, family, organisation or a country depends on the vision it has for its future growth. The leadership of an organisation takes great pains to draft these documents, keeping in view the vision for the next decade or so.

Most corporate success stories are also the stories of individuals at the top. Their dynamic and vibrant leadership emanates from a steely resolve to deal with people at all levels in the best possible manner. Former US president Harry Truman said: "Men make history and not the other way round. In periods where there is no leadership, society stands still. Progress occurs when courageous, skillful leaders seize the opportunity to change things for the better." In Helen Keller's words: "The most pathetic person in the world is someone who has sight but has no vision."

How focus is important to achieve anything in life?

Achievers have the remarkable ability to focus on whatever they do; they are completely absorbed in their work with great passion. It's because of this absorption that Archimedes ran naked through the streets yelling "Eureka", when he found the solution to determine the gold content in the king's crown. He was killed eventually when he failed to notice an enemy soldier standing in front of him, while being engrossed in solving a mathematical problem. It was this passion that led Isaac Newton to think he'd already eaten dinner while he hadn't touched a single bite.

Some go to great lengths to achieve what they set out to do. Poet Emily Dickinson literally confined herself to her house for many years and restricted her contact with other people so that she could reserve her energies for her poetry. Such behaviour isn't typical, but the point is that great achievers have always kept their goal in their sights.

2. Planning and preparation

Someone once said "leadership is the capacity to frame plans which will succeed and the faculty to persuade others to carry them out in the face of all difficulties." Another good quality of a leader is that he is always prepared for the tasks ahead and plans accordingly. This includes strategic planning, developing skills and competencies and acquiring the materials and resources they need.

Ferdinand Magellan was a great explorer and navigator. He educated himself and learned geography, astronomy, navigation and other skills that would be required in his future endeavours. He went to the cities that had the libraries and the people he wanted to meet. He arranged the finance and spent considerable time recruiting an able crew, getting ample supplies, and supervising the loading of his ships. Most good writers do a lot of research before they begin writing. Music composers listen to great symphonies by famous composers like Beethoven before they create memorable music. Inventors and scientists read volumes on the work already done in their fields and then work ceaselessly to accomplish something new. Military leaders do intensive studies, make strategies, arrange weaponry and manpower and familiarize themselves with enemy territory, troop plans and their strategies. No detail is too small for the achiever's attention. Good preparation is the first step in the right direction.

3. Conviction and a belief in themselves

Another great feature of good leadership is that they have great faith in themselves and believe in what they do. Composers Wagner and Debussy were ridiculed for their early efforts, but they kept on composing as they firmly believed that they were on the right track. Abraham Lincoln strongly believed in human dignity and decided to abolish slavery even when threatened by secession by more than half the states in the USA. Martin Luther King continued fighting for civil rights for blacks in the USA even after his house was bombed several times and he himself was attacked. They got their courage from a conviction that their beliefs were based on values and they could do no harm to any person.

Everyone believes in the power of nature, God, or a subconscious. We all must have empathy with others' beliefs, since it's the only way to live and operate in a diverse and heterogeneous society. True faith can move mountains and creates a Gandhi, an Edison, a Lincoln, an Einstein or a Buddha. Faith and belief lead to wisdom; egos are then dissolved, wandering ceases and we reach a perfect state of joy, happiness and blessedness. A few years back, I visited the Tirupati temple in Andhra Pradesh to offer my prayers to Lord Venkateswara. This temple attracts millions of pilgrims every year. Most people get their heads shaved after prayers. When I asked some of them why they went through such rituals, they said it completed their worship, removed stress and dissolved their egos. During the Kumbha Mela that takes place every 12 years, millions of people take a holy dip in Ganga and other rivers in one of the biggest congregations in the world. The worshippers believe that the holy rivers will wash their sins away.

Undoubtedly faith and belief can work wonders. But

sometimes questioning our beliefs can give us new insights. Till 1954, nobody thought an athlete could run a mile in less than four minutes. Medical experts had declared that it was not humanly possible. However, a medical student, Roger Bannister, decided to have a go at that elusive benchmark as he had already done three-quarters of a mile in less than three minutes. He succeeded. And thereafter a large number of athletes have broken the four-minute barrier. It's just that one has to break the mental barriers first before one breaks the physical barrier.

4. Persistence, perseverance and resilience

Most winners have to go through physical and emotional suffering and overcome the biggest of difficulties. What keeps them going? The answer to this question can be summed up in two words: persistence and perseverance. Their endurance is exemplary, they develop the capacity to work very hard and their physical and mental stamina is awesome. Their ability to persist in their efforts, in spite of hardship, constraints, and opposition make them legendary figures.

Painter Vincent van Gogh was too poor to afford even brushes, but he painted beautifully without them. In 1860, Louis Pasteur discovered a cure for rabies. While he was working on developing the vaccine, his three daughters died but these monumental tragedies never stopped him from carrying on with his work. Thomas Edison was a maniac for work and used to work nights too, taking small naps in between. The great painter and sculptor Michelangelo was so immersed in his work that once he skipped eating and sleeping for many days despite a severe backache. The only thing he wanted to do was paint. Days later, when he took off his socks, his skin too came out with the socks. Alexander the Great fought even when he was badly wounded many times.

These achievers faced multiple obstacles on their way to the goals they had set. They failed a lot of times but had the resilience to bounce back again. When they made mistakes and failed, they regrouped and tried again. Their success lay in the fact that they didn't accept failure. Such people treat life as a learning experience and failure as an opportunity to improve. Most inventors accept failures as an integral part of the creative process. It is an undeniable fact that we feel depressed when we meet obstacles and face setbacks. But real winners assess the situation and bounce back with new vigour and vitality. If such achievers didn't have such tremendous resilience, would we have heard about them?

5. Innovation, creativity and inventiveness

Only those who are receptive to great ideas are creative. They are prepared to capitalize on their intuitive powers, and stimulate creativity in themselves and others. We shouldn't think of creativity as being associated only with those in the field of arts; people who can paint pictures, write books, or compose symphonies. Creativity exists in every mind in abundance. To be creative means to be flexible and imaginative. It's the ability to work around problems, to find solutions and to experiment with new techniques and approaches. Why do organisations have brainstorming sessions? Because they unleash creativity and bring out amazing ideas. A human brain has two spheres — the left sphere and the right sphere. While the left sphere deals with logic, words, analysis and sequential thinking, the right side deals with creative and intuitive thinking, pictures and synthesis.

Henry Ford used his creativity to become the first industrialist to develop the assembly line, which was used to produce automobiles in his factory. He held brainstorming sessions and chose good ideas for his operations. Great rulers like Alexander the Great, Julius Caesar and Napoleon were known for their innovative battle strategies. They pioneered techniques that had never been used before in warfare. Creativity enables us to use innovative ideas and put them to work, making it a potent weapon to venture into unknown and uncharted territory.

New inventions and discoveries can be made only by thinking differently. Gregor Johann Mendel carried out his legendary experiments on garden peas from 1857 to 1865. He possessed a very logical brain and worked on his experiments with great precision. His conclusions are now known as Mendel's Laws. His work is treated as a classic in genetics for its elegance and simplicity, and ranks among the most outstanding contributions of all time. American statesman and scientist Benjamin Franklin's curiosity about lightning led to conduct the famous experiment with a kite; with his practical sense, he went on to devise the lightning rod to protect buildings. Alexander Fleming's curiosity about a new type of fungus he had found in his dish led to the discovery of penicillin.

Surprisingly, not all achievers are highly educated. Knowledge, innovativeness and inventiveness have nothing to do with formal education. Man's inventiveness can overcome the greatest of constraints. Thomas Edison, for instance, never had a proper school education. Gurudev Rabindranath Tagore had very little formal education but that didn't stop him from being a creative genius. Besides being a Nobel-prize winning author, he was a man of many talents. Good education definitely leads us on to the path of knowledge but that may not be enough, or even necessary. Great sages, writers and inventors have proved it time and again.

6. Courage and risk-taking ability

One cannot become a winner without showing great courage. Since time immemorial, man has demonstrated the grit and determination needed to overcome challenges. If you have the desire, the knowledge and the will to act, you can do whatever you want. It had always been the dream of men to fly like a bird. When the Wright brothers came up with a new machine that was capable of flying through the air, people mocked them. But they were silenced when they saw the result. One only has to see all the scientific achievements and discoveries that were achieved to realize that one can do wonders provided one has the courage. The great scientist Marie Curie once said: "Nothing in life is to be feared; it is only to be understood."

Mahatma Gandhi's contribution to India's independence is a magnificent example of courage and character. He realized that the British Empire was too powerful to be tamed by force, and decided to confront it with the power of non-violence and truth. No matter how strong a force, if it is not based on fundamentals it cannot withstand the power of truth. There's no doubt that the battle with the British Empire was prolonged, but in the end it was the truth that won. Gandhi's courage gave him the capacity to weather the storms he had to face during the freedom movement. Albert Einstein said about Gandhi: "Generations to come will scarcely believe that such a one as this walked the earth in flesh and blood."

Winston Churchill said: "Courage is rightly esteemed the first of human qualities... because it is the quality which guarantees all others." I have found in my experiences with people that a majority of them don't want to come out of their comfort zones. They are content with their lives and are not willing to take risks and break conventions. They develop fears about practically everything and don't want to gamble with their reputations, careers, health and finances. They live according to old and outdated paradigms; their rigidity envelops their character and they become complacent. On the other hand, good leaders venture into unknown territories, thriving on taking risks. They are not afraid of the consequences.

Socrates knew about the consequences of telling the truth. He dared to confront the authorities and was forced to drink poison and end his life. Dante suffered banishment as his writings had offended the political class of his time. Both Copernicus and Galileo suffered when they stated that the sun was the centre of the universe, and not the earth as it was believed to be. But both were confident that they were right, since their theories were based on facts. Charles Darwin also faced tremendous resistance to his theory of evolution. The great navigators Columbus and Magellan sailed into unknown waters to find new lands. All these people were willing to exchange security for knowledge, discovery, and understanding.

7. Good leaders are team players; they empower and delegate

When two or more people come together for a common purpose, objective or cause, they make a team. Teams are seen everywhere, be it a family, business, government organisations or the community. Can you climb a mountain or peak by yourself? It's not possible. You need a team because the task is too big to be handled by a single person. It's better to understand the formation of teams in a structured manner.

People in the workplace often talk about building a team, working as a team and so on, but few understand how to build, develop and nurture an effective team. Belonging to a team, in the broadest sense, is a result of feeling part of something larger than yourself. It involves understanding the mission or objectives of your organisation or specific team project.

In a team-oriented environment, you become an integral part of a group and contribute to the overall success of the organisation. You work in tandem with team members and coordinate with the other teams in the organisation to produce desired results. Even though you may have a specific job function in a particular section, you are united with other members of the organisation in accomplishing its overall objectives. The larger objective drives your actions; you form a part of the bigger picture or the larger objective of the organisation.

More than two decades ago, B.W. Tuckman maintained that small teams move through five stages of development: Forming, Storming, Norming, Performing and Adjourning.

Stages of team development:

Forming: A team is formed and explores what works for it and what does not. This is a period of orientation and acclimatization.

Storming: At this stage members of the group or team become more comfortable with one another and assert their individual personalities. Sometimes members become hostile and fight ground rules to operate the group or team.

Norming: At this stage conflicts that arose during the previous stages are addressed and group unity emerges. Goals, norms and rules are established and the group acts as a whole.

Performing: Structural issues are settled or resolved and the group begins to act as a unit. Team members direct their energies towards a common goal or objective. This way the structure of the group supports and eases group dynamics and performance.

Adjourning: Group wraps up activities, such as task forces formed for specific objectives.

Based on the objectives, two kinds of teams or groups — formal teams and informal teams or groups — can be observed. Formal teams are deliberately created by managers inside business organisations and have specific tasks to help the organisation achieve its goals. For instance, command teams, committees, task forces or project teams. Informal teams or groups are created for events like company picnics or outings, and provide a good opportunity for employees to know each other.

Can you imagine a team without a leader? A leader is as good as his team members. He has to maintain a balance between the needs of the task, maintaining the team and the needs of individual members. These are three circles that intersect with each other. A leader must strive to maintain all three needs. He has to see that the interests of the individual members do not clash with those of the team. At the same time, he has to respect individual needs too. The right balance has to be created to unleash creative energies.

Core functions of team leaders:

- Defining the task or objective
- Planning
- Organising
- Briefing
- Controlling

- Evaluating
- Motivating
- Getting feedback

Good leaders believe in empowerment and delegation. But can there be empowerment without trust? Trust is the binding factor in relationships and occupies the prime slot in team-building too. It helps individuals manage conflicts in families, organisations and communities. If there is no trust, there is no empowerment. When the level of trust is very low in an organisation, structures become heavy and there are tighter controls. On the other hand, in organisations where there is more trust, people in general take responsibility and enjoy a greater degree of freedom. Giving freedom in places where the trust level is very low might be detrimental to the healthy growth of individuals or organisations as some loose cannon might take advantage of the freedom.

US President Theodore Roosevelt once said: "The best executive is the one who has sense enough to pick good men to do what he wants done and self-restraint enough to keep from meddling with them while they do it." Increased responsibility helps individuals to use and unleash their creativity, talent and intelligence. It helps them to be more confident and willing to take initiative. Delegation also speeds up the decision-making process. Another US president, Ronald Reagan, said: "Surround yourself with the best people you can find, delegate authority, and don't interfere as long as the policy you've decided upon is being carried out."

A good leader is also an assertive leader. We express our will by being assertive. It means that we have the right to exist and also to express who we are and what we want, while accepting the fact that other people have an equal right to their own existence. Assertive people are moderate, open, warm, trusting, solution-finding and empathetic. They are effective communicators and listeners. Mahatma Gandhi, Nelson Mandela and Abraham Lincoln are examples of such people.

Passive people on the other hand avoid confrontation and are shy and submissive. They are quiet, hesitant and defensive, don't take pride in themselves and give in easily. They lack courage and conviction and are always in a confused state. Most losers can belong to this category, barring those who dared and lost.

Aggressive people believe in the theory of 'I win, you lose'. They want to win even at the cost of other people. They are concerned mostly with their own needs and are not bothered what other people want. They are quick to blame others and are authoritarian by nature. Most dictators belong to this category.

Passive-aggressive people are a hybrid of the two. They are tight-lipped, impatient and make sarcastic comments. They lack confidence but use aggression to hide the fact. People with little knowledge, who are only interested in appearances, belong to this category.

Good leaders belong to the assertive category. They never leave their team members in the lurch. They give credit to team members when they win and take the blame when things go wrong. They respect individuals, create harmony and manage conflicts effectively. Tension or anxiety is the result when needs or desires are frustrated or thwarted. Inter-personal conflicts arise when individuals or groups encounter different viewpoints. Conflicting views cause tensions.

Conflicts arise when:

- **The goals of two individuals or groups are incompatible.**
- **People in a team or group have diametrically opposite values.**
- **People have conflicting ideas or thoughts.**
- **People have incompatible feelings or emotions.**
- **People act in a way that's unacceptable to others.**

But conflicts are not always bad. Some conflicts are a must as they introduce dynamism; maintaining status quo all the time will lead to the demise of organisations. Sometimes people must give vent to their anger, feelings and emotions. If there is no conflict or tension, there won't be place for any innovation, creativity and inventiveness in organisations. Two teams or departments with conflicting ideas may together come up with new ideas that could be beneficial. Conflicts, however, must be handled tactfully or they could snowball into a major problem. Management-union conflicts are quite common in most organisations.

Let me illustrate the team-building exercise and leadership with the example of the Oscar-nominated movie Lagaan.

Learning from Lagaan

This epic movie is about a tiny village in 19th century India ruled by a local king, who is under British control. The village and its surrounding areas are badly hit by a prolonged drought. While the villagers suffer, the exploitative and oppressive British live an opulent life.

Despite the drought, the British decide to double the lagaan (farm tax). The poor villagers — who can't manage two square meals a day — find themselves hard pressed to pay these exorbitant taxes. The British officers meanwhile play cricket and party every evening. The local king, who asks the British to reduce the tax, is humiliated by them. When Bhuvan, the hero of the film, opposes this, the British increase the farm tax by three times, posing a threat to the very survival of the poor villagers. Bhuvan is then severely criticized by the villagers.

The British then make an offer to Bhuvan: if his team of villagers beat the British officers in a cricket match, there would be no tax for three years. Bhuvan takes up the challenge, even though the game of cricket is Latin and Greek for him and the others. But he doesn't get any support from the villagers, who are reconciled to their fate and feel they can do nothing against the mighty British regime.

Bhuvan uses his powers of persuasion and convinces the villagers that it is much better to fight the oppressive regime rather than to surrender meekly. He gets help from an unexpected quarter. The sister of the British governor, spotting the potential in Bhuvan, gives him and the villagers valuable tips in playing the game. And despite all sorts of problems, Bhuvan puts together a team. His efforts pay off: the movie ends with a great victory for Bhuvan's team, which wins the villagers a three-year reprieve from taxes.

Bhuvan took up the challenge though he lacked the expertise to beat the British in their game. But he was clear in his objectives and that clarity provided him with strength and direction. With clarity in vision, one can overcome any obstacle. He had immense confidence in dealing with challenges and adversity, and the capacity to organise and motivate people. Moreover he had the power of truth and courage on his side.

We can identify with the character of Bhuvan. All of us

face challenges and adversity like Bhuvan, but somehow not many can generate the passion needed to overcome them.

In the context of business organisations, managers and other staff explore novel ways of improving profitability. It doesn't matter what you call team-based improvement efforts or strategies — continuous improvement, total quality, re-engineering, or work teams — you are striving continuously to improve results for internal and external customers. But sometimes these efforts don't produce the desired results. A thorough diagnosis of the problem is then required. Successful teams always concentrate on certain essentials in effective team-building. Before we discuss the essential elements of effective team-building, it's essential to ask a few questions.

- **Why do so many team-building exercises, seminars and meetings fail to enthuse participants?**
- **Why does leadership fail to define the larger objectives on which teams would be based?**
- **Why does leadership fail to develop an overall sense of teamwork in its members, which is different from building an effective and focused work-team?**

Essential elements of good team-building:

Clear context and expectations: There should a clear understanding by team members as to why they are in a team. Do they understand how the team would help the organisation realize its business goals and organisational goals? Understand where it fits in the larger picture and whether they feel aligned with the organisation's goals, principles, vision, mission and values? Team members need to understand well the team's reporting relationship or structural hierarchy. Do they hold each other accountable for project deadlines, commitments and results? Does the organisation have a strategy or plan to create new opportunities for self-management among its members?

It's necessary for the leadership to clearly communicate its expectations about the team's performance and expected outcomes. This includes a clear understanding as to why the teams have been formed. Ask whether there is a defined review process to ensure that both the team and the organisation have the same direction and purpose? It would help in defining the purpose.

Team understanding: There has to be a clear understanding of team process and development. Team members should understand the roles and responsibility of other team members. This helps in problem solving, process improvement, goal setting and measurement. There should be effective conflict resolution, consensus and decision-making. Dos and don'ts should be established and roles clearly defined. The requirements of the team should always take precedence over individual needs.

Communication: Are team members clear about the priority of their tasks or objectives? Is there an established system to receive honest performance feedback? A clear understanding of the context and a transparent information system help in the team-building process. Team members should communicate with clarity and confidence with other members and the team leader. A good leader must be a good communicator. Good and honest communication helps resolve conflicts.

Creativity, innovation and inventiveness: These are key to good team building. Change compels individuals and organisations to think differently. Ask yourself if your organisation is really interested in change. Does it value creative thinking, unique solutions and new ideas? Does it have a system to reward people who take reasonable risks to make improvements or does it reward people who just fit in and maintain the status quo? Does your company strive to be a learning organisation and provide the necessary inputs to keep it thriving and prospering?

Consequences and end results: Do the members of your team feel responsible and accountable for team achievements? Are rewards and recognition systems in place? Does your organisation and leadership respect and encourage risk-taking abilities, or are team members always afraid of punishment? Is your organisation ready to share the rewards and blame? Do team members recognize their impact on the organisation's success?

Coordination and creating cultural change: A central leadership should assist groups in obtaining what they need for success in a coordinated manner. That is, it should prioritize and allocate resources. It also should have a clear understanding of cross-functional and interdepartmental synergy. Team building works best in a collaborative, empowering, enabling atmosphere, which is distinctly different from the traditional, conservative and controlled atmosphere. It's the culture of the organisation that determines future growth. Does it respect its employees' creativity, energies, values, beliefs and faiths?

Commitment: Do team members want to participate in the team? Do they feel that its needs are more important than their own? Are members committed to accomplishing the team mission? Do they feel that their contribution to the cause is as valuable to the organisation as it is to their personal careers? Does the atmosphere at work encourage the development of competencies? Are team members excited and challenged by the team opportunity?

8. Integrity and belief in values

There is a time in the life of every man when he is confronted with ethical dilemmas and has to take a stand. This is the time when one's faith in universal principles is tested to the utmost. During such times of trial, one can do the wrong things to get material comfort and prosperity. Or one can stick to principles and do what is right and accept great misery. Abraham Lincoln once said: "Nearly all men can stand adversity, but if you want to test a man's character, give him power." Character is the sum total of all truths. Great characters make great people, and shape the destiny of civilizations.

The best leaders are those that have strong character. John Adams said: "The people have a right, indisputable, unalienable, indefeasible, divine right to that most dreaded and envied kind of knowledge — I mean of the character and conduct of their rulers." Great people draw their strengths from true faith and belief. Their lives are based on a changeless core. Their truths are universal in nature and they never try to manufacture their own. These persons have tremendous belief in their mental abilities.

All great people are pathfinders. They never curse the darkness; they always light a candle. They lead people in the face of great challenges and adversity and sacrifice their own lives rather than let their people down. Their faith in an inner conscience strengthens their resolve.

Just turn the pages of history and check for yourself how many people, through the ages, achieved greatness without paying a price. They all had to face huge challenges, and converted adversity into opportunity. They gave meaning to their lives through their selfless service. They became symbols of truth, character and integrity. Mark Twain warned: "Keep away from people who belittle your ambitions. Small people always do that, but the really great make you feel that you, too, can become great."

Someone once said: "No one ever finds life worth living — one has to go out and make it worth living." Luminaries like Gandhi, Lincoln, Jesus, Buddha, Mahavira, Krishna, Vivekanand and Nanak are regarded as lighthouses of wisdom. They were the fountainhead of all virtues. Their message of love, compassion and brotherhood was eternal, crossing continents and enlightening mankind. According to R.C. Samsel, "Character is the firm foundation stone upon which one must build to win respect. Just as no worthy building can be erected on a weak foundation, so no lasting reputation worthy of respect can be built on a weak character." True character and integrity are the hallmarks of a great man.

How does one learn to be responsible? Abraham Lincoln said: "I neither ask nor desire to know anything of your plans. Take the responsibility and act, and call on me for assistance." All visionaries have these things in common: they never ever compromise, they are trustworthy and they have impeccable integrity. They take the responsibility and act according to their conscience, working relentlessly for the masses. They sacrifice their comforts for the sake of mankind. Bruce Barton said: "Nothing splendid has ever been achieved except by those who dared to believe that something inside them was superior to circumstance."

Aaruni's duty

Aaruni, the son of Rishi Aruni, was one of the students at Rishi Dhoumya's ashram. He was assigned the task of looking after the fields and the animals at the ashram.

Aaruni found that because of the undulating nature of the land, a lot of soil was being washed away from the fields during the rains, thus reducing the farm's productivity. He discussed the problem with his Guru Dhoumya, who told him to level the land and build an embankment wall all around the field. Aaruni worked hard and completed the task.

When the rains began, Dhoumya asked Aaruni to check whether the wall was holding out. At one place Aaruni found a breach, which threatened to become bigger unless prompt action was taken. He tried to plug the breach then and there but could not do so. As a last resort, he lay down across the breach to check the flow of the water. Soon, the soil carried by the flowing water was deposited on his body and the wall was saved.

That evening when Aaruni did not return to the ashram, Dhoumya got worried and went out along with a few of his other students to look for Aaruni. When they reached the field they found Aaruni lying across the breach, numb with cold. The sage's anxiety gave way to joy. With great pride he embraced Aaruni and congratulated him for having done his duty even at the risk of losing his life.

(Courtesy : Honey Bee Journal)

John F. Kennedy inspired a whole generation in the sixties with his words: "Ask not what your country can do for you, but what you can do for your country." According to George Gritter, "A duty, which becomes a desire, will ultimately become a delight."

Good leaders are assertive and humble at the same time. They respect human dignity and strive to get equity and justice for all. In India, we greet each other by saying 'Namaste'. Nam means to bow; As means I and Te means you. Together they form the word Namaste. It is a sign of humility, meaning "the divine in me bows to the divine in you." Compassion gives our lives meaning. Mahatma Gandhi said: "A life of sacrifice is the pinnacle of art and is full of true joy."

Compassion is the outcome of true dharma, and makes us understanding, caring and forgiving. A compassionate person makes others feel valued and motivated. When we understand people and respect their emotions, they respond positively. A compassionate attitude also leads to peace and happiness. Loretta Girzartis said: "If someone listens, or stretches out a hand, or whispers a word of encouragement, or attempts to understand a lonely person, extraordinary things begin to happen." On the contrary, if you show apathy and remain aloof, you create mental barriers that could cause stress.

When negative pride or ego takes over the mind, you seek only power and control. You spend a lot of energy chasing the mirage of material wealth and block your natural intelligence and energy flows. This only leads to disharmony, exploitation and conceit and cause agony and pain. It can seriously get in the way of a noble life. The story of Narada from Indian mythology aptly illustrates this dilemma.

Narada's pride

Sage Narada was the son of Lord Brahma, creator of the universe. He had the divine powers to go anywhere in the universe. He loved the Gods and the Gods also loved him very much. He could meet the lords of the universe, Brahma, Vishnu and Mahesh, at will.

One day he felt that there was no one in the universe who loved the Lord as much as he did. So he asked the Lord: "Is there anyone who can love the Lord more than

I?" But the Lord was not amused and told Narada: "There's a greater devotee of mine in this village on earth. Go and meet him." Narada was surprised to hear this. He could not believe that someone could love the Lord more than him. Nevertheless, he went to the village and inquired about that particular villager. The villager was a farmer and thought of God before he left for his fields. He worked all day and prayed again before going to bed.

Narada thought: "How can this farmer love God more? He works all day and utters His name only twice, whereas I think of the Lord at every moment." When Narada complained to the Lord about this, the Lord listened carefully and said: "Narada, take this cup filled to the brim with oil, and go all around the wall of heaven and come back. But see that not a single drop is spilt." Narada thought that wasn't too difficult. He was very careful and came back triumphantly without spilling a drop.

When he reported the matter to the Lord, the Lord asked Narada: "How many times did you remember me while you were going around the wall of heaven?" Narada was amazed to find that he had not uttered the Lord's name even once while going around the wall. His entire concentration was on successfully completing his task. The Lord said: "So you forgot me completely while carrying this cup of oil. But that poor farmer worked on his field every day religiously and remembered me twice a day. Now you tell me who loves the Lord more." Narada acknowledged his mistake and thanked the Lord for reminding him of the evils of excessive pride.

A commitment to core values is an outstanding characteristic of visionary leaders. Committed leaders follow an inner sense of direction, and lead from the inside out, as Mahatma Gandhi did. Gandhi said: "I must first be the change I want to see in my world."

Many successful business leaders, such as Narayana Murthy of Infosys, have demonstrated the importance of sticking to the right values; in fact Murthy's values have contributed to Infosys' profits and standing in the IT sector. He says his people are his greatest assets and maintains that a company has an equal responsibility to the community. A study by Curtis Verschoor published in Management Accounting a few years ago found that companies with a commitment to ethical principles do better financially than those that don't.

Our effort should be to bring our value system in harmony with true principles. It is my experience that whenever we try to defy the law of nature we lose. This story of the sun and other living creatures summarizes the true principles.

The Sun and the Rooster

All creatures were unhappy with the intensity of the Sun. They felt the world would be a much better place without this fireball and complained incessantly about its heat and brightness. The Sun continued to perform his ordained task though he was furious. The complaints, however, grew stronger and one evening the Sun was asked to pack up and go and never return. He did exactly that. The next day, the Sun did not rise. All the creatures were delighted; they slept long and undisturbed through the everlasting night. However, when the Sun did not rise for the third consecutive day, they began to feel uneasy. All creatures, except a few that had stocked their food stores, grew hungry, as they could not find food in the dark.

It was not long before they began to despair. Hunger made them lose their tempers and they began to accuse each other of bringing on the disaster that had befallen them. Despite all the bickering, saner voices prevailed. It was decided that emissaries must be sent to placate the

Sun and get him back. The best of birds, beasts and men set forth on their mission. They begged the Sun to return. But the Sun, who was still feeling hurt and insulted, refused. “Go away and don’t bother me,” he said. The great ambassadors of peace came back crestfallen. Another emergency meeting was held. This time, the Rooster was selected as emissary. He was a non-controversial animal. Besides, he was harmless, polite, good looking, diplomatic and most of all, persuasive.

He spruced himself and went to meet the Sun. On reaching the Sun’s house, he addressed him thus: “O mighty Sun, you are the most wonderful of God’s creations. You have done well to others without expecting anything in return. We small creatures are foolish. We lack the foresight that you have. If we have made you unhappy out of our sheer foolishness, will it be just for you to punish us? If we were wise like you, we would never have complained as we did. We have realized our blunder and are genuinely sorry for it. In fact, a number of small creatures, including myself, did not share the decision of asking you not to return to the earth. But we were in the minority: our voices were ignored. As a result, my tribesmen are vanishing at an astonishing rate because the wild cats are feasting on our hens and chicks. Please come back. I will announce to the whole world each day as you return that the Sun, our life-giver, is returning in all his beauty, majesty, dignity and warmth. Similarly in the evening before dusk, I will announce your departure. Hereafter, the dew will fall on the ground and the flower will open at dawn as a token of respect to you when you rise over the horizon. All the creatures expect you to grant our prayer and are eagerly awaiting your return.”

On hearing these words, the Sun was moved and replied: “If there were only a handful of creatures like you, I would certainly return, but alas, that is not to be.” The shrewd bird gauged at once that the Sun was more than half-willing to return and he pressed on further saying, "Oh mighty Sun, unless you return soon all the small creatures that form the bulk of creation will perish."

The Sun then smiled and consented to return. All the creatures rejoiced to hear this news. The Rooster became the hero of the day. True to his promise, the Sun returned and rose in splendour the next day. And the Rooster kept his word. He got up early and announced the Sun's arrival in his clear, loud voice. He was ready again that evening to usher out the Sun. And so it is, till today, that the Rooster heralds the Sun's arrival and departure each day.

This tale highlights our tendency to take nature for granted.

Courtesy: Naga Folk Tales by Luikham R, 1983, Ref: HB vol. 5(2), April-June 1994.

Such stories compel us to rethink and remodel our lives. They teach us to live in harmony with nature and not to waste precious energies on futile dreams.

9. Independence and commitment

Good leaders are self-reliant. Never was Shakespeare's famous quote "To Thine Own Self Be True" truer than in the case of the great men and women who followed their own hearts, and not the expectations of others. Others' opinions or acceptance did not regulate their lives; neither did they affect their behaviour and ideas. Good leaders are independent and free thinkers. They free themselves from patterns that are comfortable in order to do new things. They go beyond the call of duty and eschew rigidity.

George Eliot is a good illustration of an independent person. Though she was a woman, Eliot dared to enter into a literary career at a time when it was a man's domain. Emily Dickinson confined herself to a room to write poetry that surged from her heart like the waves of an ocean. Despite criticism she vehemently refused to change the style of her poetry. Impressionist painter Vincent van Gogh set up home in the country where he felt he could work best. Writer Leo Tolstoy defied all conventions by giving up his material possessions and founded a commune. They were not discouraged by what people said, and continued to do things their own way.

It was also their positive mental attitude and commitment to their cause that made them legendary figures. It was because they had a sense of purpose in their lives. Take the case of Abraham Lincoln, who stated many times that his role during the Civil War and in uniting America was one in which he was only a vehicle for God's work. Winston Churchill too spoke about his role in leading Britain to victory in World War II in similar terms. Mahatma Gandhi maintained that his political work arose from his obedience to the will of God. Because of their higher sense of purpose, many of these historical giants were in reality very modest people. They didn't think of themselves as being great. True success comes only when you commit to excellence in whatever you do. All that is required is a slight edge over your competitors.

These qualities had always existed in human beings. Although we perceive modern civilization as being advanced, with people having greater intellect, talent and courage compared to past generations, the fact remains that people before us were also as great in their own environment.

Good leaders believe greatly in creating a purpose in life.

In organisations, this purpose is reflected in mission statements. Mission statements state the purpose of a company's existence, and to be fair must deal with the needs of all stakeholders. If a mission statement deals with just one particular need or stakeholder — that is, earning money for owners — it is faulty, incomplete, partial and perhaps erroneous. Mahatma Gandhi said: "If you are right in one department of life but attempting to do wrong in another, you are still wrong as life is one indivisible whole and everything affects every other thing. It is inter-related." Life is like an ecosystem and a mission statement must deal with all means and ends, all needs, all stakeholders and must be used as the constitution by all people at all levels in the organisation. A mission statement must satisfy physical, social, mental and spiritual needs.

Gandhian view on leadership: The topic of leaders and leadership would not be complete without examining Mahatma Gandhi's philosophy. Gandhi's thoughts on truth and non-violence are eternal and universal and it was his firm belief in these truths that made him a Mahatma (Great Soul). His beliefs like removing untouchability, trusteeship, respect for all religions, non-violence, compassion, love and humility for all have made him unique. Gandhi spoke about ethics in public life at great length. According to him, there were seven deadly sins — related to the social, political and spiritual fabric — that destroyed communities and nations.

Wealth without work: Some people reap what they have not sown. Mahatma Gandhi equated this to stealing. It is consumption without sacrifice. If you are using material objects without earning them honestly, you are stealing them. Such people resort to politics, manipulation, deceit, cheating, forgery and other wrongful means to get what they want. They are not concerned about the pain they inflict on the community; for them gains take precedence over pain. These mentally bankrupt people create and establish systems and structures that result in frauds, scams and forgeries. They come up with new schemes to rob innocent people of their hard-earned wealth. Favours, prejudices and biases take the place of sanity.

The Gandhian philosophy of trusteeship deals with all stakeholders. It calls for fairness and benevolence towards all stakeholders — employers, employees, suppliers, distributors, consumers and the community as a whole. Gandhi felt that trusteeship would transform the idea of wealth and the relationship between the individual and the community. Aditya Vikram Birla, J.R.D. Tata, Narayana Murthy and Azim Premji are examples of people who created wealth through honest and ethical means.

Pleasure without conscience: If life were all pain or only pleasure, there would be no romance. Just think of our immense joy when there's a new birth in a family. We also get great pleasure in things like watching wild animals in a forest reserve, sunrise and sunset, chirping of birds, flowing river water, the sound of conches on the bank of the river Ganges etc. Life is a mission, a constant journey. When we achieve our goals, we feel happy and satisfied. The pleasure that one gets through selfless service is the real thing. But in this material world, where ends take precedence over means, pleasure seekers become parasites. Take the example of pornography, where physical pleasure at any cost is the prime motive, while women are exploited to the hilt. Character and integrity are lost to sensuousness. How would you describe such sub-humans? Parasites with physical bodies, bereft of soul. These persons are like cancerous cells, which infect and destroy all the healthy cells in a body.

Take the case of camel races that were held in some Gulf countries. Small children were tied on top of camels and their cries and screams made the animals run faster. Thousands of people enjoyed these races but at what cost? Many children died in the process and others got mentally and physically crippled. This brutality smacks of the Middle Ages. How can people behave like animals? The British regime exploited poor Indians for more than two centuries. It was brutal and people were subjected to all kinds of atrocities. The British rulers lived in great opulence while their local subjects were dying of hunger and disease. Most colonies suffered a similar fate.

Knowledge without character: When Abraham Lincoln was an attorney, someone once asked him to take up his case. Lincoln studied the case thoroughly and refused to plead for him. The case was technically strong, he said, but ethically and morally it was wrong and he was not going to take it. Lincoln was a man of very high character and integrity and he could not bear to lie in a court of law.

Most developing nations are very poor, with a woefully inadequate infrastructure. There is a wide gulf between the haves and the have-nots. The poor have neither access to free medical treatment nor can they afford to pay exorbitant medical costs. The United Nations Charter treats all people equally and recognizes the basic rights of all citizens. But we are living in an imperfect world and great disparities do exist. A large number of professionals from diverse fields get involved in mal practices. It has also been observed that some of these professionals decline to lower their fee for the cause of poor or in the larger interest of Community. Such people work for their own selfish ends. Caring, empathy and compassion don't find any place in their lives. They are nothing but a drain on society. In the words of Gandhi, these people live a compartmentalized life. Knowledge, if not complemented by character and integrity, is nothing but wickedness. Ms Indu Puri, chairman of Bennett, Coleman and Co, says: "Learning without wisdom is incomplete. Wisdom that doesn't give rise to feelings is incomplete. Feeling that doesn't translate into action is incomplete. And action that doesn't give rise to fullness is incomplete... for fulfillment is returning to the self — the source." Lord Krishna says in the *Gita*: "True knowledge dispels the darkness of ignorance and illumines the whole world."

Business without ethics: Gandhi emphasized a lot on the importance of ethics and purity in personal and professional life. His theory of trusteeship is the direct outcome of the ethical thought process, and maintains that wealth should be generated and distributed in such a way that it benefits the majority of people. Ethics and hard work always complement each other. Our professional lives revolve around the manufacturing and service sector, generating a lot of wealth and opportunities. But it's how we generate it that matters the most.

During the past few decades, we have seen a huge increase in nefarious business activities through which individuals and organisations have succeeded in getting rich quick. They have defrauded thousands of investors of their money through phony schemes, leading to stock exchange crashes. Billions of dollars all over the world have been lost. Systems have been subverted and established norms violated with gay abandon. Huge bankruptcies, commercial frauds and scams marked the end of the last millennium. The events of 11 September 2001 were a direct attack on the monuments of capitalism. The year 2002 saw the collapse of another set of twin towers — ethics and morals — in the corporate sectors of the world. The commercial frauds were the result of colossal human failure, and their effects were felt all over the world.

When morals and ethics are relegated to the back alley, such outcomes become inevitable. When greed takes the prime seat, most stakeholders suffer. Service and sacrifice become alien words and personal agendas flourish at the cost of virtues and the good of society. Wealth and power achieved through such means are short-lived, but cause a lot of damage.

Science without humanity: We are living in a world of technological marvels, be it in communication, transportation or other fields. New scientific inventions and discoveries have made our lives comfortable. Man has invented things like huge flying machines to minimize distances. Mahatma Gandhi was aware of the power of science, having witnessed the industrial revolution in the West. Every scientific innovation, he believed, must revolve around the welfare of human beings, and must benefit the masses. If people die of diseases despite the availability of medicines and expertise, it is a blot on humanity. Sacrifice, compassion and human values should be at the core of scientific development. Gandhian philosophy touches the very core of total human development. It is holistic and total.

Mahatma Gandhi also decried the destructive use of science. Along with material comforts, science has also created weapons of mass destruction. Who can forget the horrific bombing of Hiroshima and Nagasaki?

Religion without sacrifice: The ancient Indian scriptures lay great emphasis on sacrifice: it is the noblest of deeds, loved by the Lord, and is key to a just society. Sacrifice means helping others even at the cost of oneself. All the world's religions emphasize on sacrifice. Any religion that does not preach sacrifice is not a religion. The hardened religious tendencies that have come to the fore in the last few decades do not conform to the true essence of any religion. It has caused immense harm to the harmony of the community. People have been killed in the name of religion and it does not augur well for the future. The need is to understand and practice religion in the right spirit.

India is the land of saints. Vivekanand, Tukaram, Namdev, Chaitanya Prabhu, Dyaneshwar, Kabir and many others have spread the message of love, compassion and sacrifice. These saints travelled the length and breadth of this country and worked tirelessly to promote a composite culture, which was based on respect for other religions, sects and faiths.

Politics without principles: Why does a system degenerate? Why do people lose faith in a system? Systems get subverted when power and wealth are limited to a few people, and organisations and states are ruled like personal fiefdoms. Favours, biases and prejudices become the order of the day. Established governments are uprooted for ulterior motives, morals are mocked at and unscrupulousness governs social behaviour. Relationships weaken and the community degenerates into the dark ages.

The twentieth century has seen phenomenal advancements in science and technology but there has been no psychological change that would work as a catalyst for a new world order based on mutuality and universal principles. Mahatma Gandhi was greatly concerned about the falling moral standards in politics. According to him, principles apply to all men at all levels. A principle that tends to vanish or leads to destruction or does not hold good should be regarded as invalid. The law of dharma — righteousness, compassion and right action — is true for all times.

There is a dearth of good leadership:

History is full of examples of leaders whose selfless service guided the destiny of many organisations and states. If George Washington and Abraham Lincoln were synonymous with American freedom and democratic polity, Gandhi stands for India's freedom struggle. Lincoln was credited with a new system of governance — government by the people, for the people, of the people — a paradigm shift at that time; Gandhi on the other hand fought with the help of an imperishable weapon: the power of truth and non-violence. The Gandhian philosophy of non-violence inspired great leaders like Nelson Mandela, Martin Luther King and many others.

There is no doubt in my mind that there is a dearth of good leadership around the world. Moreover the lust for power and money is taking deep roots in many organisations and countries. Even big corporates are getting infected by this menace. People preach freedom but practice control, preach democracy but support autocracy, preach selfless service and practice total selfishness. They work to pursue their own personal goals and cause irreparable damage to the social fabric. It is sad but true that psychologically we have neither grown nor learnt any lessons from history. Probably we cannot get out of the habit of creating a mess around us time and again.

Max De Pree rightly said: "The first responsibility of a leader is to define reality. The last is to say thank you. In between, the leader is a servant."

The Chinese philosopher Lao-Tzu, in the sixth century before the Christian era, defined leadership as:

A leader is best
When people barely know that he exists,
Not so good when people obey and acclaim him;
Worst when they despise them.
Fail to honour people,
They fail to honour you.
But of a good leader, who talks little,
When his work is done, his aim fulfilled,
They will all say, 'we did this ourselves'.

ACTION SHEET

List the qualities you look for in an ideal leader:

1.

2.

3.

4.

5.

What leadership qualities do you have?

1.

2.

3.

4.

5.

Which leadership qualities do you lack, but would like to develop:

1.

2.

3.

4.

5.

CHAPTER 6

MOTIVATION: THE SPARK THAT IGNITES ACHIEVEMENT

It was 1982. Steven Callahan was determined to cross the Atlantic Ocean in his sailboat. During the course of his voyage, his sailboat hit something and sank — he was adrift on a small lifeboat far away from shipping channels with limited supplies. His chances of survival looked bleak. However, Callahan did survive; he was rescued 78 days later, alive though much skinnier. His survival is a fascinating story of surmounting impossible odds.

Callahan managed to keep himself going when everything seemed lost, even when his rubber lifeboat got punctured and he was badly dehydrated. It was his will power that enabled him to survive. Callahan wrote: "I tell myself I can handle it. Compared to what others have been through, I am fortunate. I tell myself these things over and over, building up fortitude..." Such people make history.

Sir Edmund Hillary and Tenzing Norgay were the first to climb Mount Everest on 29 May 1953. Earlier, in 1952, Hillary had attempted to climb the highest peak in the world but failed. But while addressing a public meeting a few weeks later, he moved to the edge of the platform and made a powerful announcement: "Mount Everest, you beat me the first time, but I'll beat you the next time because you've grown all you are going to grow... but I'm still growing."

Why do people want to climb Mount Everest? Why do

they want to take huge risks to achieve something extraordinary? I know many people who have achieved excellence in academics, sports, business and other streams of life and sometimes I wonder at their level of motivation and passion. They have the strong urge to be a winner, and want to accomplish something different. What makes them do so?

What is motivation?

Our actions and behaviour are directed by our psychological and physiological needs. They make people put their efforts and energies into what is desired. But how far they succeed depends on the levels of motivation. People may have the necessary skills but their effectiveness depends on motivation. Motivation is a powerful force and drives people to do extraordinary things. It is an inner urge or a burning desire that makes life dynamic and vibrant. People with a high level of motivation are full of energy, enthusiasm, determination, and are high performers. They seek cooperation and are always willing to lend a helping hand. They face challenges with a smile. Motivation is the key to peace and happiness provided it is in a positive mould. It can literally change one's life.

Motivation begins with a need, vision or dream to achieve the seemingly impossible. It's the unfulfilled needs that work as activators; satisfied needs don't motivate any one. Research has shown that it's not possible to attain personal and organisational goals if there is no enduring commitment from members of families or organisations.

Akio Morita, the founder of Sony Corporation, began his career as an entrepreneur in the ruins of a Japan devastated by World War II. He was highly motivated, and also recognized how important it was to keep his employees motivated. In his autobiography, he emphasized on the need for a leader to hire competent co-workers. He wrote: "No matter how good or successful you are or how clever or crafty, your business and its future are in the hands of the people you hire." Morita established a lifetime employment system, giving employees incentives to stay on with the company. He died in 1999, but his legacy survives. It has motivated and will continue to motivate people to think and act differently.

Motivation can be either internal or external. Recognition, money, job enrichment, social approval, fear and fame are external motivators. Pride, sense of achievement, responsibility and self-belief are internal motivators. External motivation is temporary and disappears the moment its motivator goes away. Internal motivation is permanent since it is the product of the inner core.

Motivators that affect us:

1. Money.
2. Job enlargement:
   (a) Task variety.
   (b) Meaningful work modules.
   (c) Ability utilization.
   (d) Performance feedback.
   (e) Job enrichment (added responsibility).
3. Quality of work life.
   (a) Adequate and fair compensation.
   (b) Safe and healthy environment.
   (c) Avenues for developing skills and competencies.
   (d) Growth avenues and security.
   (e) Protection and respect for employees' privacy, dissent and equity.
   (f) A sensible integration of job, career, family life and leisure time.

(g) Acceptable hours of work.
(h) Acceptance and recognition.
(i) Challenges.
(j) Rewards.
(k) Good job design.
(l) Benefits.
(m) Promotions and transfers.

4. Sense of achievement.
5. Sense of pride.
6. Societal approval.
7. Responsibility.
8. Fame or fear.
9. Self-belief.

A high level of internal motivation leads to passion, an intense desire to achieve something. It represents the ultimate devotion to a goal and the ensuing single-mindedness. Passion ignites dormant talents that enable us to do exceptional things. Great achievers in any field have intense desires, high motivation and passionately pursue set objectives.

The ability to inspire and motivate employees separates exceptional leaders or winners from ordinary leaders. In a recent study, researchers at the University of Nebraska-Lincoln examined sources of motivation among Nebraska's workers, both in urban and rural settings. The results concluded that there are five sources of motivation.

1. **Fun, which is an intrinsic motivation.**
2. **Rewards**
3. **Reputation**
4. **Challenges**
5. **Setting goals or a purpose in life**

Good leaders will find innovative ways of motivating people. Those who tap into just one or two sources would motivate only a fraction of their workers and be less effective.

Types of motivation

Incentive Motivation: Some people or managers believe that employees have to be paid money, provided trips, prizes, titles, stock options and so on to keep them working and motivated. "Eat your food and you can have dessert" is how parents use such incentives on their children.

There is a problem with this kind of motivation. Think of the classic example of the donkey pulling a cart with a carrot dangling in front of him. Now this method would be effective only if the donkey is hungry enough, the carrot sweet enough, and the load light enough. If the donkey is not hungry, this ploy won't work. The carrot has to be sweeter and bigger or you will have to wait until the donkey is hungry again. A drawback of incentive motivation is that it is purely temporary and external. Besides, an organisation may not find it sustainable, since employees may demand more and more.

Fear Motivation: Threatening, firing and demotions are some ways in which organisations get work done by employees. Parents too use fear tactics to keep children in line. To recall the donkey analogy we used in the previous paragraph, it's like using the whip on the animal to pull the load. In this case, either the donkey will become nervous and jumpy or he will become used to such treatment and cease to fear it. Similarly, fear when used on people works for some time before it loses its effectiveness. If fear is used for long periods, it might lead to stress and illness among employees.

Attitude Motivation: This is the most important type of motivation. Here you don't need carrots, whips or someone to guide people's actions. They are motivated internally and behave like well-trained racehorses and not load-carrying donkeys. Here people are independent and take their own decisions, which are based on the strategic directions of the top management. This type of motivation is internal and permanent and a direct outcome of the thinking and conditioning process.

This is a story of twin boys who were totally different by nature. One was an optimist with a positive mental attitude while the other was a sad and hopeless pessimist. Concerned about their divergent natures, their parents decided to take them to the local psychologist. The psychologist then came up with a plan to balance the twins' personalities. While the pessimist twin was put in a room full of fine gifts, toys and many other beautiful things, the optimist twin was given a box of manure. The parents were asked to observe the behavioural pattern of the twins. When they peeked in on the pessimist, they heard him audibly complaining: "I don't like the colour of this toy... I'll be sick if I eat these chocolates... It is a horrible game... I know other children have a bigger toy car than this." He was finding fault with virtually everything around.

Thereafter the parents decided to take a look at the optimist and saw him gleefully throwing the manure up into the air. He was jumping with joy and saying: "With this box of manure, there's got to be a pony around!" Look at the difference. While one who has everything is making a mess of it the other is making the most of the situation. With a "can-do" attitude, one can easily sustain a higher level of natural motivation.

Achievement Motivation: Here, people derive their motivation from a sense of achievement. They seek to enhance their existing standards of performance by setting up higher benchmarks. These people are eager to know the results of their efforts. When people set higher goals for themselves, they are motivated to achieve them. When mountaineers set their sights on the highest peaks in the world, they are motivated by a feel-good factor. They are not bothered by the problems they face, and their goals become an obsession. Most inventors, adventurers and entrepreneurs have this mental state.

How do you help people in your organisation change their attitudes and behaviour? Here are some questions you should ask:

- **Does your organisation have a positive mindset towards its people?**
- **Do you undertake programmes to develop people at all levels within the organisation?**
- **Have the capacities of your people been put to the test or do they remain grossly under-utilized?**
- **Are enough opportunities being created to motivate your people and use their energies, potentials and capacities?**
- **Are specific goals being set to prioritize things? Is the performance of employees being acknowledged and rewarded?**
- **Is there an atmosphere of problem-solving inside the organisation? Are problems being actively tackled or are they pushed under the carpet?**
- **Do you develop inter-personal skills and encourage people to communicate in an effective manner?**
- **Do people have an empathetic attitude and listen to others attentively, understanding each other's needs and requirements?**

- **Does your organisation have a clear strategic direction based on the mission statement? Or are they just placards on the walls?**
- **Do people at all levels feel they are an integral part of a team or organisation?**

Fredrick Herzberg came up with a very popular theory of motivation, called the two factors theory or motivation-hygiene theory. He carried out a survey of 200 accountants and engineers, who were asked to answer two questions:

When did you particularly feel good about your job?

When did you exceptionally feel bad about your job?

The responses were interesting. Certain characteristics tended to be consistently related to job satisfaction while others were related with dissatisfaction. Intrinsic factors such as achievement, recognition, the work itself, responsibility, advancement and growth seemed to be conducive to job satisfaction. These were called Motivators Satisfiers and Job Content Factors. When they felt good about their work, the respondents tended to attribute feel-good factors to themselves. On the other hand, when they were dissatisfied they tended to attribute it to extrinsic factors such as organisational policy, administration, supervision, working conditions, salary, status, security and inter-personal relations. These factors were called Dissatisfiers, Hygiene Factors, Maintenance Factors or Job Context Factors.

According to Herzberg satisfaction and dissatisfaction are not opposite poles of one dimension; they are two different dimensions. While satisfaction is related to motivators, dissatisfaction is caused by hygiene factors.

The need hierarchy of motivation propounded by social scientist Abraham Harold Maslow is undoubtedly the simplest and most widely discussed theory of motivation. Maslow maintained that there exists a hierarchy of five needs within every human being. These needs begin at the lower levels and go upwards as lower-level needs are satisfied. Let's see this need hierarchy:

1. **Physiological needs:** Include hunger, thirst, shelter, sex and other bodily needs.

2. **Safety:** Includes security and protection from physical and emotional harm. Most readily observed in infants and young children because of their relative helplessness and dependence on adults. In the organisational context, job security, salary increases, safe working conditions, unionization, lobbying for protective legislation, pension schemes, provident funds, gratuity, insurance, grievance-solving procedures, system of seniority, lay-offs etc are safety factors. Other instances when safety needs arise are during times of war, crime, floods, earthquakes, riots, social disorganisation and natural calamities.

3. **Love and belongingness:** These needs include affection, belongingness, acceptance and friendship. In the organisational context, these represent the need for a compatible work group, peer acceptance and professional friendship.

4. **Esteem:** These needs belong to a higher level and are felt when lower-level needs are satisfied. It includes factors like self-respect, autonomy and achievement, status, recognition and attention, prestige and appreciation.

5. **Self-actualization:** This is the highest need in Maslow's need hierarchy. It is all about achieving one's full potential. It means making full use of one's

capacity, potential and talent. In reality this need is never satisfied.

This theory or hypothesis was widely criticized by social scientists for being incomplete, partial or perhaps erroneous. In his last days, Maslow renounced the need for self-actualization. He said that the meaning of self-fulfillment doesn't mean just personal growth and satisfaction. In reality this need must deal with overall prosperity and happiness of people around you. He admitted that his theory was not complete.

How to motivate people in an organisation:

- Managers should cope with satisfiers and dissatisfiers.
- Improve hygiene factors.
- Provide satisfiers.
- Be more realistic.

Signs of motivation:

- High performance and consistent results.
- Energy, enthusiasm and determination to succeed.
- Unstinting cooperation in overcoming problems.
- Willingness of individuals to accept responsibility.
- Willingness to accommodate necessary changes.

Signs of lack of motivation:

- Apathy and indifference to the job.
- A poor record of coming on time or absenteeism.
- Low energy levels, criticism and unwillingness to deal with problems and disputes.
- Lack of cooperation in dealing with problems or difficulties.
- Undue resistance to change.

Most people are capable of achieving remarkable things if they are given the right inputs and motivational leadership. Of course, it's not easy to motivate people who are totally beat-up, fatigued and cynical. People with low motivation are found in every organisation. An atmosphere needs to be created to inspire them; here, the role of leadership comes in handy. All team members need to be assessed by the team leader without any prejudices, biases and preconceptions. Leadership must create linkages among people to create positive synergy. Here are some ways of motivating people:

Treat people on merit: Different people think and behave differently. They have specific motives and perceptions, likes and dislikes, and must be treated accordingly. A shy person, for instance, can be given a job that requires him to work alone. A talkative person, on the other hand, could be better placed in sales and marketing. Good leadership always provides a lot of free time to its people and recognizes performance. As a leader, use incentives to motivate people in your team. Remember, your approach has to be unique to each individual. Also, set realistic but challenging goals for the workforce.

Never wait until annual or periodic appraisals to speak about staff performance. Communicate to people on their shortcomings. Find out what demotivates them. Discuss work-related problems and identify their causes, whether due to stress, emotional problems or physical sickness.

Set major goals but follow a path: Our life is an indivisible whole with different compartments — family, career, social, health, psychological and spiritual. To keep ourselves motivated, we must set goals in all areas. Set mini-goals in each area and accomplish them. Accomplishing small goals will get you into the habit of setting bigger goals for yourself.

Finish what you've begun: Some people are in the habit of leaving jobs half-finished. Quitting is a negative habit and won't take you far in life.

Don't fear failure: Failures, learn from them and the resilience to bounce back are essential elements of motivation. No one has achieved success without failures. Most success stories are also the stories of great failures. Don't be upset by minor problems. Let them roll off your back.

Create a purpose in life: If you don't know your destination, you are heading for your demise. Create a purpose in your life to remain alive and vibrant. A purpose gives your life value and meaning.

Create passion in your life: It is passion that makes a difference to the lives of individuals, families and organisations and not structures, strategies or management systems. Have you ever noticed the passion in Tiger Woods' eyes when he is playing golf? He is so focused and energetic. This man thinks of golf every waking moment.

Nature too shows its passion in the form of lofty heights, roaring waterfalls and swift-flowing rivers. Passion is a force that fills life with courage, meaning and joy. It calls on us to act, and fosters commitment, determination and discipline in our lives. Passion can be either constructive or destructive. An individual guided by violent passions can be devastating to humanity. What Osama Bin Laden did was the outcome of a destructive passion. But when such passion is directed towards good and fair objectives, it leads to a better and meaningful life. Passion drives people to do extraordinary things; it is a flame and a burning inner urge that can ignite the inner soul.

Passion enables us to explore frontiers that had never been explored before. It is what motivates inventors, discoverers and adventurers. It helps us become what others are afraid to become. It helps us look beyond what is possible.

Have you ever noticed the high energy levels small children seem to have? They get easily excited because they have little fear in their minds. They are extremely curious, and can barely contain themselves when their incessant questions are answered. They pop like a freshly opened champagne bottle. If their love is intense their outrage is equally strong, and they don't have any inhibitions about expressing either. In the organisational context, an environment that doesn't create enough passion kills creativity. In such an environment, it won't take much time to convert a thoroughbred horse into a donkey. As adults we need to learn from children as to how to create and sustain a high level of energy and drive.

The 21st century will be known as the century of knowledge. It offers tremendous opportunities for leaders who are willing to take the initiative and understand and cultivate passion among their people. Management gurus Jackie and Kevin Freiberg say employees must ask themselves three questions to cultivate a proper career development programme:

1. What are my gifts and talents?
2. What am I passionate about?
3. What needs to be done?

Here's what they have to say: "When people can answer

these questions clearly and the answers intersect, they become passionate about what they do. Few things are professionally more fulfilling than doing work that you are extremely good at and turned on about. It's an incredible feeling when what you're good at and excited about enables you to make a contribution that truly adds value to the business and its customers! Work ceases to be a vocation and becomes an avocation or a passion."

The 21st century poses multifaceted challenges in the community we live in. These challenges revolve largely around relationships either in business or in the family environment. In this era we will need to have passion and not be afraid to ask tough questions in our search for the best answers.

Some questions Jackie and Kevin Freiberg ask:

- Are we working on things we're truly good at?
- Do our people go home at the end of the day emotionally charged or emotionally drained?
- Will the projects we are working on today be remembered five years from now?
- Are we proud of the work we do?
- Does the cause for which we fight go beyond making money and increasing market share?
- Does it create any meaning in our lives?

"If we can truly answer yes to these questions, we can cultivate the kind of passion that enable us to live more fulfilling lives, lead courageously, engage in work worth bragging about, and stride boldly into a future of our own choosing!" is what they say.

Simply believe in yourself and see things start happening to you!

ACTION SHEET

1. Do you set organisational goals to motivate your people?
2. Do you set new standards of performance?
3. Do you provide regular training to your staff?
4. Do you recognize performance and reward people?
5. Do you encourage new ideas given by your staff?
6. Do you value people's potential and capacities?
7. Are you passionate about life and its processes?
8. Do you work as a catalyst to ignite the feelings of your fellow workers?

What kind of person are you?

Someone who watches things happen.
Someone to whom things happen.
Someone who doesn't know what's happening.
Someone who makes things happen.

Former US president Dwight Eisenhower said: "Motivation is the art of getting people to do what you want them to do because they want to do it."